STEVE

South West
Mountain Biking

Quantocks • Exmoor • Dartmoor

Design and production by Vertebrate Publishing, Sheffield
www.v-publishing.co.uk .

South West
MountainBiking
Quantocks • Exmoor • Dartmoor

Written by
Nick Cotton & Tom Fenton

Photography by **John Coefield**

South West
MountainBiking
Quantocks • Exmoor • Dartmoor

VG Copyright © 2011 Vertebrate Graphics Ltd, Nick Cotton and Tom Fenton.

VP Published by Vertebrate Publishing
First edition published 2005. Second edition published 2011.

ISBN 978-1-906148-26-3

Front cover photo: Will Wykes climbing back out of Smith's Combe in the Quantocks.
Back cover photo: John Horscroft riding through Hound Tor on Dartmoor.

Photography by **John Coefield** unless otherwise credited.

  All maps reproduced by permission of Ordnance Survey on behalf of The Controller of Her Majesty's Stationery Office.
© Crown Copyright. 100025218

 Design by Nathan Ryder, production by Jane Beagley.
www.**v-graphics**.co.uk
Printed in China.

 MIX
Paper from responsible sources
FSC® C016973
www.fsc.org

Contents

ROUTE GRADES
▲ = MEDIUM ▲ = HARD ▲ = EXTREME (see page xi)

Introduction

Dartmoor, Exmoor and the Quantocks offer some of the finest mountain biking in England, comparable in quality and variety with anything you'll find in the National Parks of the north.

Dartmoor's scenery is unlike anything else in the country, with strange shaped grey granite tors rising up out of the landscape; streams cutting deep through dingly dell valleys where you expect pixies to be hiding behind every rock and a bleak, grassy moorland plateau as remote and unforgiving as parts of the Pennines - all riddled with tracks and trails to test every ability.

By contrast Exmoor is smaller and more intimate with a denser network of byways and bridleways criss-crossing the moor. The variety is even greater as Exmoor offers rides high up above the coast as well as tracks over high heather moorland, climbs and descents to make your heart sing and a plethora of pretty villages with pubs and tea shops to satisfy the hungriest appetite. A speciality of the region is the rollercoaster stone stream beds - punctuated with serial drop-offs, they get better each time you ride them.

The Quantock Hills are quite extraordinary - less than 10 miles long and 4 miles wide, they pack in well over a hundred miles of trails on well-drained tracks through gorse, heather and woodland from the broad and easy ridge trail to excellent testing twisty singletrack. Very much a place to explore over and over, perfecting your own circuits as you work through the myriad options.

So, take your pick, explore, enjoy and tell your friends!

Nick Cotton

Acknowledgements

We would like to say thank you to a few people:

A big thanks to Tom Fenton for giving the Quantocks section a complete overhaul and for re-riding and rewriting the routes: we're now pretty confident we've got the best (legal) Quantocks rides out there! Thanks to Will and Helen Wykes, Gwynfor Jones, Abigail Elce, Neil McEwan and John Horscroft for being such great photo models and to John Coefield for his work in photographing them. Thanks to Tim Russon for the extra Dartmoor photos. To Jane Beagley at VP for producing the guide, and thanks to all the team at Vertebrate Graphics and Publishing for their support.

How to Use This Book

Riding on Dartmoor

Dartmoor has a fascinating mixture of moorland, forest, dramatic granite tors, dingly dell pixieland and old mysterious stones. The mountain biking varies from tangles with tussocks on the high moorland to superb stone-based tracks and everything in between. Despite being much larger than Exmoor, Dartmoor has fewer mountain biking options as there are vast swathes of grassy plateau in the centre where there are no tracks, and other places where a bridleway marked on the map may not correspond to anything on the ground!

Do not despair! There are enough tracks around the edges of the moor, and also around the Princetown/Postbridge area in the centre, to offer a great selection of rides to test the fittest of riders.

In the north and west the rides explore the edges of the moor from Okehampton, Lydford and Peter Tavy, all of which could be linked up for a mega day out. The one exception to the fringes of the moor rule is the military road loop which climbs right into the heart of the moor to 560m. Although this is also used by the occasional vehicle, it has a very different feel to it from a 'normal' mountain bike ride.

In the centre, the bleak grey prison town of Princetown is a hub for two rides: down to Burrator reservoir and across open moorland past the atmospheric ruins at Swincombe to Hexworthy. A little further east, one ride from Postbridge explores Bellever Forest and crosses rivers via some potentially side-splitting stepping stone crossings. A second ride from Postbridge goes past the ruins of the medieval village of Challacombe across hillsides laden with ferns and heather. This could easily be linked to the two rides based around Manaton and North Bovey for another big day out. The Grimspound ride is an old favourite, taking in the incredible shapes of Hound Tor and more dingly dell streams and boulders.

The final ride is in the southeast: the ride from South Brent taking in Avon Dam reservoir has a series of fast grassy descents that will bring a grin to anyone's face.

Riding on Exmoor

Square mile for square mile, Exmoor is surely the best National Park in the UK for mountain biking – can anywhere else boast such quantity, quality and variety of trails? Routes up on the cliff tops with views across the Bristol Channel to Wales; intimate wooded combes with twisting, testing rooty singletrack; remote moorland that could easily be compared to that in the Peak District or further north; and then there is the speciality of the region – rollercoaster bedrock descents with enough drop-offs to test the keenest mountain biker. There really is something on Exmoor to suit every rider.

12 rides are described on Exmoor and it would not be impossible to find 12 more, such is the quantity of well-maintained bridleways, byways and RUPPs (Roads Used as Public Paths). The rides in the north are dominated by the coastal views: from Lynton and the Valley of Rocks in the west through to Selworthy Beacon in the east, the tracks take you high along the cliffs with wonderful coastal views. The central rides touch on rough and rugged moorland; some of these rides are best savoured as experiences of raw elemental nature, not as a challenge to break personal best times. They are a chance to blast away cobwebs and the occasional wind-battered tree will show how effectively that will happen.

The principal villages of central and southern Exmoor - Exford, Winsford, Simonsbath, Withypool, Dulverton and Wheddon Cross - can all be linked together by interlocking rides enabling you to do two, three or even more routes in a day if the conditions are right and you are feeling fit and up for it. Porlock is the other obvious centre to the north of the region with several rides nearby and easy access to almost all of the moor.

Dunkery Beacon and Tarr Steps

Exmoor National Park has specifically requested us not to promote rides in these two areas, in order to avoid exacerbating user conflict. They are very popular with walkers, and, as there are so many bridleway alternatives in the park, the request does not seem unreasonable. Think of them in the same light as the voluntary restrictions on Snowdon: you have every legal right to use the bridleways in the area but try to avoid times that are busy, particularly summer weekends.

Riding in the Quantocks

The Quantocks. Where every track is a bridleway, every bridleway is singletrack and every singletrack is a little twisty, turny bit of heaven. OK, technically that might be a slight exaggeration. But it doesn't feel like one. Enjoy: it's hard not to.

If you've not ridden the Quantocks, we're almost jealous of you, because you're in for a treat. Small, but definitely perfectly formed, their diminutive size and wandering wild ponies give them a friendly feel. Get up onto the tops and you'll find a view that stretches across the Bristol Channel into Wales. And, more immediately, you'll also spot a multitude of singletrack bridleways twisting and tumbling into the wooded combes below. Technical enough to make you concentrate, but never so much that you stop grinning and start worrying, they pretty much guarantee a good ride.

But let's not get carried away here. The Quantocks can't be perfect. For starters, you're not allowed to feed the ponies. There aren't enough cafés. And... well... nope, that's it.

The Routes

This guide contains the best routes in the South West (in our opinion!). The aim is to encourage you to ride new trails in new areas, and to help you get to know the region. Try the routes as suggested, in reverse or joined to neighbouring rides. Once you've ridden a few and got to know what's what, you'll be able to link sections together to create your own rides.

Grades

Routes, climbs and descents are graded blue, red and black, in a similar system to that used at trail centres around the UK.

▲ = Easy   ▲ = Moderate   ▲ = Hard

Blue graded routes are generally shorter routes and are within reach of most MTBers, even newcomers, as well as the kind of thing you could do in a short day or when the weather's really foul. **Reds** are the kind of rides that won't actually take a full day, but you'll probably not want to do anything else once you've ridden them. And **Blacks** are those big and memorable days out that will demand endurance and some technical ability in places. These are the kind of routes to work up to.

The grades are based on average conditions – good weather and not too wet and muddy. In a drought the routes will feel easier, in the depths of winter, harder. Grades consider technicality, length, climbs, navigation, and remoteness – so one 'black' route might be a short all-out technical test while another could be a big endurance challenge with tricky navigation. As ever, these grades are subjective. How you find a particular route, downhill or climb will be dictated by your own levels of fitness and skill.

Directions & Accuracy

While every effort has been made to ensure accuracy within the directions in this guide, things change and we are unable to guarantee that every detail will be correct. Please treat stated distances and times as guidelines. **Please exercise caution if a direction appears at odds with the route on the ground. A comparison between direction and map should see you on the right track.**

Rights of Way

Countryside access in the UK hasn't been particularly kind to cyclists, although things are improving. We have 'right of way' on bridleways (blue arrows on signs) and byways (red arrows). However, having 'right of way' doesn't actually mean having the right of way, just that we're allowed to ride there – so give way to walkers and horse riders. We're also allowed to ride on green lanes and some unclassified roads, although the only way to determine which are legal and which aren't is to check with the local countryside authority. Obviously, cycle routes are also in.

The very understanding Forestry Commission generally allows cyclists to use its land (again, you'll need to check with them first to be sure). You must, however, obey all signs, especially those warning of forestry operations – a fully loaded logging truck will do more than scuff your frame...

Everything else is out of bounds (unless, of course, the landowner says otherwise). Riding illegally can upset walkers (who have every right to enjoy their day) and is, in many cases, technically classed as trespass (meaning you could be prosecuted for any damage caused). Not all tracks are signed, so it's not always obvious whether that great-looking trail you want to follow is an illegal footpath or a legal bridleway. That's why it's a good idea to carry a map with you on every ride.

The Bike

Generally any half-decent mountain bike (try and avoid a '£99 Special') will be fine for riding these trails. For the harder routes, a full-suspension bike could add comfort and control, whilst a lightweight race bike might make the hills easier.

Check everything's working – especially for harder riding. You won't be going uphill fast if your gears seize but may be quicker than planned if your brakes don't work. Pump the tyres up, check that nothing's about to fall off or wear through and check that everything that should be tight is tight.

Essential Kit

Helmet

"The best helmet is the one that you're wearing". Make sure it fits, you're wearing it correctly and that it won't move in a crash.

Clothing

You need to get your clothing right if you want to stay comfortable on a bike, especially in bad weather. The easiest way to do this is to follow a layering system. Begin with clothing made from 'technical' synthetic or wool fabrics that will wick the sweat away from your body and then dry quickly, keeping you dry and warm. Stay away from cotton – it absorbs moisture and holds onto it. If it's chilly, an insulating layer will keep you warm, and a wind/ waterproof layer on the outside protects from the elements. Layers can then be removed or added to suit the conditions. Padded shorts are more comfortable, but the amount of lycra on display is down to you. Baggy shorts, full length tights and trousers are all available to match the conditions. Set off a little on the cold side – you'll soon warm up. Don't leave the warm clothes behind though, as the weather can turn quickly.

Gloves

Gloves ward off blisters and numb hands and help keep your fingers warm. They also provide a surprising amount of protection when you come off.

Footwear

Flat pedals/clips-ins – it's your call. Make sure you can walk in the shoes and that they have sufficient tread for you to do so. Consider overshoes if it's chilly.

Other essentials

As mentioned, take any necessary spares, tools, tube and pump, spare clothes, first aid kit, food and water. Stop short of the kitchen sink, as you'll still want to be able to actually ride your bike.

You'll need something to carry this lot in. We'd suggest a hydration pack, as they allow you to drink on the move and keep excess weight off the bike.

Maps

Ordnance Survey
Explorer OL28 Dartmoor 1:25000
Explorer OL9 Exmoor 1:25000
Explorer 140 Quantock Hills & Bridgwater 1:25000

British Mountain Maps
Dartmoor 1:40000

General Safety

The ability to read a map, navigate in poor visibility and to understand weather warnings is essential. Don't head out in bad weather, unless you're confident and capable of doing so.

Some of the routes described point you at tough climbs and steep descents that can potentially be very dangerous. Too much exuberance on a steep descent in the middle of nowhere and you could be in more than a spot of bother, especially if you're alone. Consider your limitations and relative fragility.

Be self-sufficient. Carry food and water, spares, a tube and a pump. Consider a first-aid kit. Even if it's warm, the weather could turn, so take a wind/waterproof. Think about what could happen on an enforced stop. Pack lights if you could finish in the dark.

If you're riding solo, think about the seriousness of an accident – you might be without help for a very long time. Tell someone where you're going, when you'll be back and tell them once you are back. Take a mobile phone if you have one, but don't expect a signal. And **don't** call out the ambulance because you've grazed your knee.

Riding in a group is safer (ambitious overtaking manoeuvres excepted) and often more fun, but don't leave slower riders too far behind and give them a minute for a breather when they've caught up. Allow extra time for a group ride, as you'll inevitably stop and chat. You might need an extra top if you're standing around for a while. Ride within your ability, make sure you can slow down fast and give way to other users. Bells might be annoying, but they work. If you can't bring yourself to bolt one on, a polite 'excuse me' should be fine. **On hot, sunny days, slap on some Factor 30+ and** ALWAYS WEAR YOUR HELMET!

In the Event of an Accident

In the event of an accident requiring immediate assistance: Dial 999 and ask for POLICE or AMBULANCE. If you can supply the services with a grid reference of exactly where you are it should help to speed up their response time.

Rules of the (Off) Road

1. Always ride on legal trails.
2. Ride considerately – give way to horses and pedestrians.
3. Don't spook animals.
4. Ride in control – you don't know who's around the next corner.

5. Leave gates as you find them – if you're unsure, shut them.
6. Keep the noise down and don't swear loudly when you fall off in front of walkers.
7. Leave no trace – take home everything you took out.
8. Keep water sources clean – don't take toilet stops near streams.
9. Enjoy the countryside and respect its life and work.

Planning Your Ride

1. Consider the ability/experience of each rider in your group. Check the weather forecast. How much time do you have available? Now choose your route.
2. Study the route description before setting off, and cross-reference it with the relevant map.
3. Bear in mind everything we've suggested about safety, clothing, spares and food and drink.
4. Get out there and get dirty.

Maps & Symbols

Ordnance Survey maps are the most commonly used, are easy to read and many people are happy using them. If you're not familiar with OS maps and are unsure of what the symbols mean, you can download a free map legend from **www.v-outdoor.co.uk**

We've included details of the relevant OS map for each route. To find out more about OS maps or to order maps please visit **www.ordnancesurvey.co.uk**

Here's a guide to the symbols and abbreviations we use on the maps and in our directions:

ROUTE STARTING POINT

MEDIUM ASCENT

MEDIUM DESCENT

ABBREVIATIONS
USED IN ROUTE DIRECTIONS

ALTERNATIVE
STARTING POINT

HARD ASCENT

HARD DESCENT

L = Left

OPTIONAL ROUTE

VERY HARD ASCENT

VERY HARD DESCENT

R = Right

STAGE MARKER

LINK TO ANOTHER ROUTE

52 ADDITIONAL GRID LINE NUMBERS TO AID NAVIGATION

SA = Straight Ahead

Haverfordwest

St Brides Bay

Milford
Haven

Pembro

St Govan
Head

Ti

Padstow

Wadebridge

Newquay

Bl

Truro

Redruth

St Ives

Probu

Cornwall

Camborne

St Just

Hayle

Penryn

St Mawes

Helston

Falmouth

Penzance

Falmouth Bay

Land's
End

Mount's
Bay

Cornwall

Lizard Point

Lizard

**SOUTH WEST
AREA MAP**

SECTION 1

Dartmoor

Dartmoor has a fascinating mixture of moorland, forest, dramatic granite tors, dingly dell pixieland and old mysterious stones. The mountain biking varies from tangles with tussocks on the high moorland to superb stone-based tracks and everything in between. Despite being much larger than Exmoor, Dartmoor has fewer mountain biking options as there are vast swathes of grassy plateau in the centre where there are no tracks, and other places where a bridleway marked on the map may not correspond to anything on the ground!

Do not despair! There are enough tracks around the edges of the moor, and also around the Princetown/Postbridge area in the centre, to offer a great selection of rides to test the fittest of riders.

SOUTH HESSARY TOR (ROUTE 4) *PHOTO: TIM RUSSON*

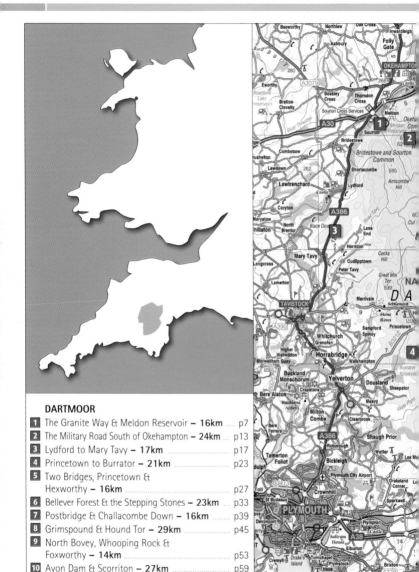

DARTMOOR

DARTMOOR AREA MAP
& ROUTE FINDER

Introduction

An easy introduction to the delights of Dartmoor, starting off with a converted railway path that is definitely a family ride, the easiest traffic-free section in the whole book, with great views out over Devon. After leaving the railway trail the going gets tougher and there is a testing stretch of singletrack and descent by the reservoir. Dodging the golf balls on the golf course at the end of the ride adds a little spice to the route.

The Ride

There can be few easier warm-ups than the railway path known as the Granite Way that runs for 8km southwest from Okehampton. As soon as you leave it the gradient steepens and the surface turns to grass and ferns with the atmospheric Sourton Tors ahead. Stone walls, grass tracks and clumps of beech trees define the route towards Meldon Reservoir beyond which the pulse quickens for a steep then easier woodland descent beneath the viaduct and on down to cross the A30. Rough pasture leads to the immaculate greens of the golf course, and tracks and lanes back to the café at the start.

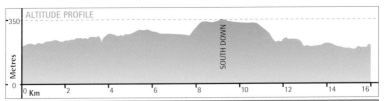

ALTITUDE PROFILE

SOUTH DOWN

Metres

0 Km 2 4 6 8 10 12 14 16

THE GRANITE WAY & MELDON RESERVOIR — GRADE: ▲

TOTAL DISTANCE: 16KM » **TOTAL ASCENT:** 180M » **TIME:** 1.5–2.5 HOURS » **START/FINISH:** OKEHAMPTON
START GRID REF: SX 593944 » **SATNAV:** EX20 1EW » **PARKING:** OKEHAMPTON YOUTH HOSTEL BY THE STATION
OS MAP: EXPLORER OL28 » **PUB:** HIGHWAYMAN INN, SOURTON, TEL: 01837 861 243 » **CAFÉ:** AT THE START

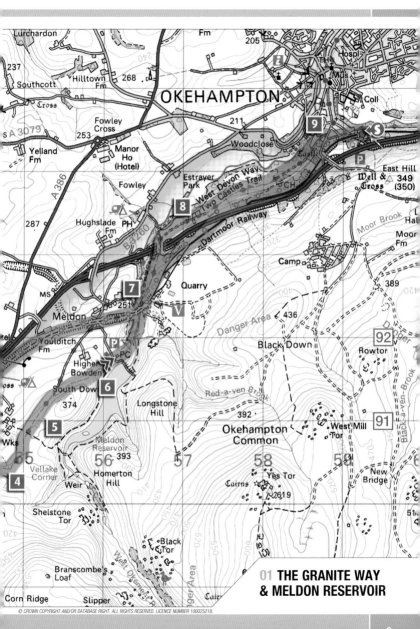

01 THE GRANITE WAY & MELDON RESERVOIR

Directions – The Granite Way & Meldon Reservoir

⮕ Exit the YHA car park, turn **R** under the bridge then take the first road **L** and shortly turn **L** again onto a zigzag track leading up to the Granite Way, running parallel with the railway line. Pass through the subway, go past old waggons and the quarry, Meldon Visitor Centre and over the viaduct.

2 Almost 8km from the start, at Sourton Church (on your right), by a green painted metal signpost, turn **R** off the Granite Way then immediately turn sharp **L** uphill to cross the bridge over the railway path. Pass through a gate and follow the middle of the stone and grass tracks uphill towards the distinctive rocks of Sourton Tors ahead.

3 There are many tracks on the ground, many of which split then rejoin. Continue in the same direction uphill. At a junction of several tracks near the top, just beneath the rocks, turn **L** on the less steep of the grassy tracks passing between ferns.

4 Go **SA** at several crossroads of grassy tracks, aiming for the clump of beech trees. Emerge from the ferns into an open grassy area then, with a wall ahead, bear **L** to join a track running alongside the wall (keep the wall to your right) leading to a wooden gate in among the trees with a *West Devon Way* waymark.

5 Go through a second gate at the end of a wide grassy track between stone walls, continue in the same direction, then at a 3-way wooden post bear **R** across the field signposted *Meldon Reservoir* to pass outside the corner of the stone wall. Follow the obvious track with the wall to your left for a short, rough section between rocks.

6 The track becomes wide and grassy with superb views. Descend to cross the road and go **SA** through a gate signposted *Meldon Viaduct*. Steep descent. **Easy to miss:** ignore a gate to the right set between two high stone buttresses then shortly keep an eye out on the **R** for a narrow wooden bridge. Cross this, then turn **L** on a wide grassy track. Descend steeply, bearing **L** to a wooden gate in a stone wall.

7 Join a broad stone track and emerge at the tarmac directly beneath the viaduct. Bear **L** downhill, keeping your brakes on, then, after 100m, bear **R** onto a narrow earth track signposted *Bridlepath*. Lovely descent on woodland singletrack. At the road turn **R**, cross the bridge over the A30 then take the first wide stone track to the **R** to the farm.

8 At the farm fork **R** then climb **R** to go through a gate and follow the path alongside the fence on your left. After a short, rough pasture section go through a gate onto the golf course, following the obvious track **SA** (watch out for golf balls!).

9 The grass track soon turns to gravel then tarmac. After 800m, at the T-junction with a more major road, turn **R** uphill then take the first road **L** (just before road signs) onto a road opposite Westhill House to rejoin the outward route. At the T-junction at the end turn **R** uphill under the bridge then turn **L** into the car park at the start.

◄☺☺ Making a day of it

The Military Road ride (page 13) also starts from Okehampton YHA. Another option: by following the Granite Way to its southwestern end, using a short section of the A386 to regain the railway path (at SX 523872), you arrive in Lydford, close to the start of the Lydford & Mary Tavy ride (page 17) at SX 502832.

02 The Military Road South of Okehampton

24km

Introduction

For a ride this long, with this much ascent, this is really an easy route, as much of the surface is either tarmac, ex-tarmac in its disintegrating stage, or broad stone tracks. As a way of climbing higher than on any other route in the book (up to a highpoint of 564m), right into the heart of the moor, it is unbeatable. Best to leave this for a day with excellent visibility as the views are very, very big. Looking through my notes I came across the following description for someone enjoying the views at the top: *Man in dark blue Astra estate with hatch up and boot full of hamster cages sits listening to the Bee Gees.* Takes all sorts, eh?

WARNING:

This ride may be shut because of firing. The firing programmes are available on the internet at **www.dartmoor-ranges.co.uk** *and on Freephone* **0800 458 4868**

The Ride

Easy woodland tracks parallel with the railway line and the A30 lead on to steep lanes up to Belstone, your only chance of a pub on the route. A broad stone track is used to continue the climb before dropping down to cross East Okement River, close to the amazingly located farm at East Okement, an outpost of bright green in amongst the wild and raw moorland. The road leads on and ever up, climbing to a highpoint of 564m. It is worth leaving the main tarmac road to cross Black a Ven Brook and follow the parallel track below Yes Tor and High Willhays, the highest point on Dartmoor (621m). Gathering speed comes with a warning! The tarmac suddenly reverts to track and it's unwise to hit this at 50kph! The one testing bit of mountain biking comes after leaving the road at Klondyke and descending to Father Ford, dropping steeply down beneath the viaducts carrying the A30 and the railway line.

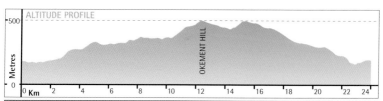

THE MILITARY ROAD SOUTH OF OKEHAMPTON   **GRADE:** ▲

TOTAL DISTANCE: 24KM » **TOTAL ASCENT**: 500M » **TIME**: 2-3 HOURS » **START/FINISH**: OKEHAMPTON
START GRID REF: SX 593944 » **SATNAV**: EX20 1EW » **PARKING**: OKEHAMPTON YOUTH HOSTEL BY THE STATION
OS MAP: EXPLORER OL28 » **PUB**: THE TORS, BELSTONE, TEL: 01837 840 689 » **CAFÉ**: AT THE START

Directions – The Military Road South of Okehampton

↱ Exit Okehampton YHA car park, turn **R** under the bridge, then just **after** a right turn to the railway station, turn sharp **R** signposted *Bridlepath to Father Ford*. Broad stone track through ferns and broadleaf woodland, gently downhill.

2 After 1.5km, just beneath the first viaduct, turn **L** over a narrow wooden bridge signposted *Okehampton via Ball Hill*. Go through a gate, join tarmac. At the road junction bear **R** then shortly take the first lane to the **R** signposted *Tordown*.

3 Climb steeply for 3km, ignoring a left turn to Priestacott. At the T-junction in Belstone turn **R** (or turn **L** for The Tors pub). The tarmac lane turns to a wide stone track at the gate.

4 After 1.5km, at a junction of tracks (by the reverse side of a *No MOD vehicles* sign), turn **L** then bear **R** to continue up the valley, at first steeply.

5 The track swings **R** downhill to cross the stream (via the ford or stepping stones). Climb. At the T-junction with a major stone track turn **L** towards tarmac. Undulating section then long steady climb to the summit, 4km after joining road.

6 **Easy to miss:** 1.2km after summit, on a fast descent and just after a 50m stretch of rougher surface, take first major wide stone track to the **L**, between stone and earth embankments.

7 Descend then climb steeply. At a T-junction turn **R** towards the tor and mast. The second summit is about 1.5km after leaving the tarmac.

8 Ignore turnings to right and left. The track turns to tarmac but comes with a **warning.** Just as you pick up speed there is a short, rough section.

9 At the T-junction by the lodge, cattle grid and bridge turn **L**. **Easy to miss:** after 1km of descent, on a sharp left-hand bend just before the first residential house, take the **right-hand** of two side-by-side bridleways signposted *Father Ford*.

10 Fast grassy descent. The trail bears **R** to run parallel with the A30. There is a steep section just after the gate. At the T-junction with a wider track turn **L** to go under the bridge signposted *Okehampton* and rejoin the outward route back to the start, following signs for Station Road.

02 THE MILITARY ROAD SOUTH OF OKEHAMPTON

Introduction

One of the easier Dartmoor rides with nothing too challenging and two excellent pubs along the way – save this ride as a treat for when you just want a gentle potter.

The Ride

The first sight of the moor at the end of the track leading up from Lydford Gorge car park may have you scratching your heads 'Where does the path go?' This is the only time on the whole ride where this will happen – at the top of the ridge ahead is the main A386 and once you are across that, it is all plain sailing. Great tracks and views east into the heart of the moor, a descent to cross the River Tavy at Hill Bridge, a short climb, an easy glide down to the Peter Tavy Inn and more good stone tracks to recross the Tavy on your way to Mary Tavy. The final hill, part on road and part off-road on grassy tracks is rewarded with wide views to the curious little church on top of Brentor, a swooping grassy descent to the road and an easy run back to the start, with the odd splash just to prove you've been out.

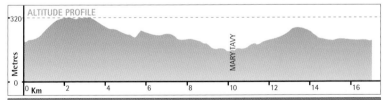

ALTITUDE PROFILE

320

Metres

0

0 Km 2 4 6 8 10 12 14 16

MARY TAVY

LYDFORD TO MARY TAVY
GRADE: ▲

TOTAL DISTANCE: 17KM » **TOTAL ASCENT**: 265M » **TIME**: 1.5–2.5 HOURS » **START/FINISH**: LYDFORD » **START GRID REF**: SX 501833 » **SATNAV**: LYDFORD (CLOSEST) » **PARKING**: LYDFORD FALLS CAR PARK » **OS MAP**: EXPLORER OL28 **PUB**: CASTLE INN, LYDFORD, TEL: 01822 820 241; ELEPHANT'S NEST, HORNDON, TEL: 01822 810 273; PETER TAVY INN, TEL: 01822 810 348 » **CAFÉ**: BRING SANDWICHES

03 LYDFORD TO MARY TAVY

❻ Exit Lydford Falls car park, turn **L** to cross the bridge and immediately turn **R** (tricky crossing on blind bend – take care) onto a broad stone track, taking the upper **left-hand** fork signposted *Bridlepath*. Climb and follow the track around to the **L** to its end.

2 Go through the field gate with a *West Devon Way* sticker and turn **R** after the first telegraph pole towards the steep slope up to your right and the obvious telegraph pole in a second line of poles. Follow a faint but wide track through gorse bushes. The track becomes more defined. Immediately after crossing a stone water channel (three large granite blocks) across the path bear **R** off the stone track onto a wide grassy track towards the road/traffic on the horizon.

3 Cross the main A386 via field gates either side of the road **SA** onto the wide stone track opposite signposted *Bridleway* (blue waymarker). Follow this ever-better stone track. At the T-junction with a wide, smooth track with a stone and earth embankment ahead turn **R**.

4 Go past a squat grey building, continuing on the main track, soon descending. At the road turn **L** (or for the Elephant's Nest pub in Horndon turn **R**) then after 200m take the first **R** signposted *Lower Creason*.

5 The tarmac turns to track and swings **L**, signposted *Bridleway to Hill Bridge*. Go through several gates and past several properties. At the road bear **R** downhill. Cross the bridge and climb steeply. At the T-junction turn **R**, signposted *Cudlipptown, Peter Tavy*.

6 Long, easy tarmac descent. **Easy to miss:** immediately after the church in Peter Tavy turn sharp **R** by Gatehouse Barn towards the Peter Tavy Inn. Bear **L** onto the lower track by the pub car park then shortly take the first track to the **R** signposted *Bridleway to Mary Tavy, National Cycle Network Route 27*.

7 Mixture of surfaces. Cross the bridge over the river, climb and join tarmac. Go past Mary Tavy church then at the T-junction turn **R** signposted *Horndon*. **Ignore** a right turn towards Horndon. Climb past the school, descend to cross the bridge, start climbing again then, on a right-hand bend by Glebe Cottage, bear **L** uphill onto a wide stone track.

8 At the crossroads with the A386 go **SA** signposted *Brentor* (take care – poor visibility). Climb gently, ignoring lanes to left and right. Cross the cattlegrid and after 100m bear **R** onto a wide stone track, soon forking **L** onto a wide grassy track signposted *West Devon Way* (blue arrow).

9 Climb, then enjoy a superb grassy descent with good views. At the T-junction with the road bear **R** then shortly, on a sharp left-hand bend, bear **R** onto a stone and grass track signposted *Bridleway, West Devon Way*.

10 **Easy to miss:** after 800m, with the house ahead about 300m away, bear **R** onto a parallel grassy track. Follow in the same direction alongside the wall and fence to your left to rejoin the outward route by the wooden field gate mentioned at the start of Instruction 2. Turn sharp **L** through this gate, descend to the road and turn **L** to return to the start.

⊶◌⊙◌ Making a day of it

To the north, a short road section will take you to Lydford and the start of the railway path that forms part of the Granite Way ride (page 7). A second option is a there-and-back ride climbing to 550m following the stone-based old tramway starting from the Fox & Hounds pub at Shortacombe up onto the moor beneath Great Links Tor. Start at SX 525866, head north to the hairpin at SX 546887 and turn around at the top at SX 555872.

HEADING TOWARDS BURRATOR RESERVOIR PHOTO: TIM RUSSON

Introduction

Is this the way forward? South of Princetown past South Hessary Tor towards Nun's Cross the National Park has solved problems of peat erosion by laying down a granite dust path. Excellent news all round, and there are even a few tricky bits for us bikers with some drainage channels across the path to test our balancing skills. What else? A teeth-rattling descent down to the lovely Burrator Reservoir and a 'How much can you ride?' climb back up to that famous granite path.

The Ride

Look at the boggy, tussocky grass either side of the improved path south of Princetown and ask yourself 'Which would I rather be riding?' Turn off westwards passing an ancient stone cross with views of the forest and the reservoir opening up ahead. Pick your line carefully and don't do this with a hangover as you'll be shaken to bits by the loose stone descent, dropping 230m from South Hessary Tor to the shores of Burrator Reservoir. The latter almost feels like civilisation, indeed as the crow flies you are only a couple of miles from the main Plymouth to Tavistock road. That ain't for us; we go back to the high moorland, through the hamlet of Sheepstor and onto the moorland track that climbs and falls then climbs again, passing the remote ruins of Eylesbarrow tin mine, the much weathered cross at Nun's Cross and back onto the superhighway leading to the bright lights of Princetown.

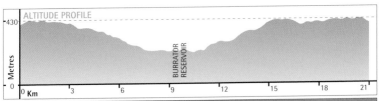

ALTITUDE PROFILE

430

Metres

BURRATOR RESERVOIR

0

0 Km   3   6   9   12   15   18   21

PRINCETOWN TO BURRATOR RESERVOIR   **GRADE:** ▲

TOTAL DISTANCE: 21KM » **TOTAL ASCENT:** 250M » **TIME:** 2–3 HOURS » **START/FINISH:** PRINCETOWN
START GRID REF: SX 590734 » **SATNAV:** PRINCETOWN » **PARKING:** MAIN CAR PARK, PRINCETOWN
OS MAP: EXPLORER OL28 » **PUB:** LOTS OF CHOICE IN PRINCETOWN » **CAFÉ:** LOTS OF CHOICE IN PRINCETOWN

Directions — Princetown to Burrator Reservoir

➏ From the roundabout at the southern end of Princetown at the junction of the B3212 and B3357 by the Visitor Centre go **SA** towards the Plume of Feathers pub car park and through the bridlegate onto a smooth stone and gravel track. Over the next 3km climb then descend, testing your skills crossing many stone drainage channels.

2 At the obvious crossroads of broad stone tracks by a 1-metre stone 'obelisk' waymarker in the middle of the path, turn **R** downhill on a similar gravel and stone track.

3 Follow this wide, loose stone track downhill for 4km, passing a stone cross after 1.2km, where views of the reservoir start opening up. Descend into coniferous then broadleaf woodland, ignoring turnings to the right. At the T-junction with tarmac turn **L**.

4 Go past the reservoir through lovely beech woodland on a quiet lane. At the road T-junction after 2.7km turn **L** towards the church (no sign).

5 Go past the church and **ignore** the first no through road to the left (by Lambs Park). Climb steeply for 750m then, immediately after crossing the cattle grid, turn **L** onto the next no through road signposted *Nattor*.

6 The tarmac ends after 1.5km just before a small wood. Pass to the **L** of the wood (and building). Ford the river or use the bridge. Climb steeply then more steadily.

7 After 2km at the fork of tracks by a ruin (low walls) bear **L** on the steeper track. The trail quality improves after 400m.

8 After 1.5km go past Nun's Cross. Go **SA** at two crossroads of tracks, rejoin the outward route and follow it back to the start.

⟜☉⟆ Making a day of it

Another ride can start from Princetown heading east to Hexworthy (page 27). The latter could link to the Bellever & the Stepping Stones ride (page 33). You may also wish to explore the old 6-mile stone tramroad around King's Tor that starts by the Fire Station in Princetown.

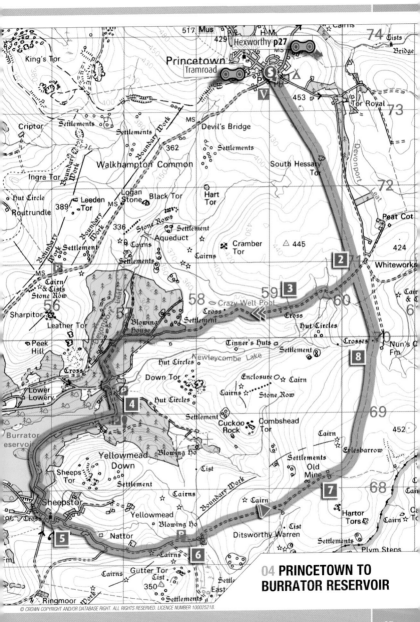

King's Tor

517 Mus
429
Hexworthy p27

Princetown
Tramroad

74 Cists
Bridge

453

Tor Royal

73

Criptor

Settlements

MS

Devil's Bridge

72

Peat Cot

424

Whiteworks

Settlements

362

Walkhampton Common

Settlements

South Hessary
Tor

Ingra Tor

Hut Circle
Routrundle

389
Leeden
Tor

Logan
Stone

Black Tor

Hart
Tor

Boundary
Work

MS

336

Stone Rows

Settlement

Aqueduct

Cramber
Tor

△ 445

Settlement

Cairns

Cairns

2

Settlement

Cairns

MS

Settlements

59

3

Cairn
& Cists
Stone Row

56

58 Crazy Well Pool

Cross

60

Sharpitor

Cross

Hut Circles

Crosses

Nun's C
Fm

Cairn
& C
6

Leather Tor

Blowing
House

Settlement

Tinner's Huts

Settlement

8

Peek
Hill

Newleycombe Lake

Hut Circles

Cross

Down Tor

Enclosure O Cairn

Stone Row

69

Lower
Lowery

Hut Circles

Settlement

Cairns

4

Cuckoo
Rock

Combshead
Tor

Cairn

452

Burrator
eservoir

Yellowmead
Down

Sheeps
Tor

Blowing Ho

Cist

Cairn

Settlements

Old
Mine

Erlesbarrow

68

Settlement

Sheepstor

Cairns

Cairn

7

Cross

Yellowmead

Boundary Work

Cairn

Hartor
Tors

Cairn

Ca

5

Blowing Ho

Nattor

Cist

Ditsworthy Warren

Settlements

Plym Stens

Fm

6

Cairns

Cairns

Gutter Tor
Cist
350

Sett
East

Ringmoor

Settlements

04 **PRINCETOWN TO
BURRATOR RESERVOIR**

05 Two Bridges, Princetown & Hexworthy

16km

Introduction

This is roof of the moor stuff, so avoid in poor visibility as you will get lost and be devoured by the Hound of the Baskervilles. I tried to extend it southwest across the featureless, tussocky grass to Whiteworks on a fine summer's day with good visibility and thought 'Mmmm, this could be very hairy in mist', hence a blast along the road to complete the loop.

The Ride

It is best to start at the bottom of the hill and get the road climb up to Princetown out of the way at the start. Farmers just about manage to eke out a living on the fields around Princetown but this soon gives way to moorland. The prevailing westerly wind and a 100m descent to the crossing of the River Swincombe should make this easy enough. What do you make of the spooky ruins at Swincombe? Hexworthy offers the chance of grub and ale at the Forest Inn or if you want to press on, head north to the extraordinary buildings of Sherberton with its unlikely saw mill. A little tricky route finding across the field at the end of the big track takes you to an ever more obvious track heading northwest to Prince Hall Hotel and the vast canopy of the beech avenue leading back to the road and the start.

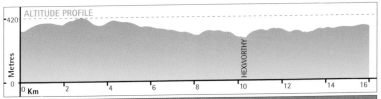

ALTITUDE PROFILE

420

Metres

0

0 Km — 2 — 4 — 6 — 8 — 10 — 12 — 14 — 16

HEXWORTHY

TWO BRIDGES, PRINCETOWN & HEXWORTHY GRADE: ▲

TOTAL DISTANCE: 16KM » **TOTAL ASCENT**: 285M » **TIME**: 2-3 HOURS » **START/FINISH**: TWO BRIDGES, NORTHEAST OF PRINCETOWN » **START GRID REF**: SX 593944 » **SATNAV**: PL20 6SW » **PARKING**: TWO BRIDGES CAR PARK, OPPOSITE TWO BRIDGES HOTEL » **OS MAP**: EXPLORER OL28 » **PUB**: FOREST INN, HEXWORTHY, TEL: 01364 631 211 **CAFÉ**: BRING SANDWICHES

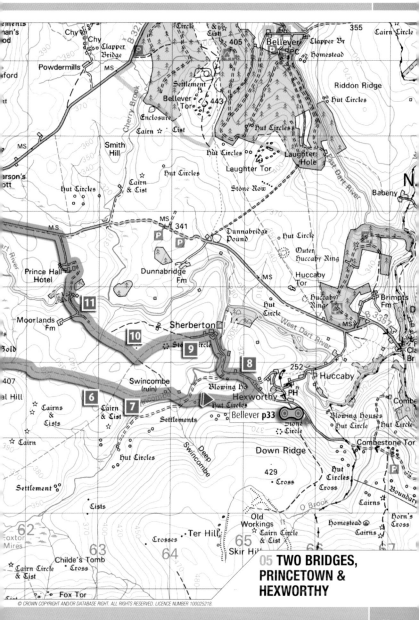

05 TWO BRIDGES, PRINCETOWN & HEXWORTHY

Directions – Two Bridges, Princetown & Hexworthy

➎ Turn **R** out of the Two Bridges car park then take the first road **L** (B3212) signposted *Princetown*. This may be busy, especially during summer holidays.

2 After almost 2km, at the start of Princetown, turn **L** after the second roadside house to the left through a gate (with a *Bridleway* sign on it) set 10m back from the road.

> **➎ Alternative Start from Princetown:** from the roundabout by the Visitor Centre in Princetown turn **L** on the B3212 towards Two Bridges. Go past Oakery Crescent on the right then, after 20m, and just before the large white house on the right, turn **R** through a gate marked *Bridleway* onto a stone track.

3 Go downhill on a stone-based track. After 1.2km cross Devonport Leat (a water channel) by a gate, then about 50m before the house and barn turn **R** towards the woodland on a broad stone track.

4 At the T-junction with a concrete track turn **L** uphill past a house to the left. Go through a field gate and continue uphill on a stone and grass track, soon taking the **left-hand** fork.

5 At the end of the stone-based track, with a reed bed ahead, bear slightly **R** to follow the obvious wide grassy track in the same direction.

6 The path undulates then runs parallel with the wall on the left. Continue in the same direction, passing a 4-way signpost on your left (you are aiming for Hexworthy). With a wall ahead turn **R** downhill for 30m then **L** through a bridlegate to continue in the same direction.

7 Go past the ruins of Swincombe, cross the wooden bridge. At a crossroads with a major stone track go **SA** uphill onto a narrow track through gorse, signposted *Bridleway*. This becomes a more obvious stone-based track.

8 At the road turn **L** (or, for the Forest Inn, Hexworthy turn **R** then after 500m turn sharp **L** at a T-junction, signposted *Princetown*). Descend to cross the bridge then climb. **Dismount** to walk through the farmyard, bearing **L** (blue waymarks/*Bridleway* signs) **before** the wood processing shed.

9 Climb, go through the gate and bear **L** away from the main stone track following closely the direction of the *Bridleway* sign. Navigation is a bit tricky: you are aiming for the top of the field at the junction of the walls to go through a metal gate by a blue-topped *Path* signpost.

10 After 300m, at a square post, turn **R** signposted *Prince Hall* towards a clump of trees in the distance. Descend to cross a small stream then climb. At the T-junction with a concrete road bear **R** downhill.

11 Cross the bridge, climb and follow *Path* signs along an amazing avenue of beeches. At the T-junction with the B3357 (may be busy) turn **L** to return to Two Bridges.

◄═OO Making a day of it
Another ride starts from Princetown: Princetown & Burrator (page 23). The ride described here overlaps with the Bellever & the Stepping Stones ride (page 33) between Hexworthy and Sherberton. Leave this ride at SX 652726, join the Bellever ride then rejoin this ride at Sherberton at SX 646733.

STEPPING STONES ACROSS WEST DART RIVER

Introduction

Is there a ride in the whole of the UK with as many stepping stone river crossings? I doubt it. This is not a ride to do during or after heavy rains but someone with a camera or video might just catch some very entertaining crossings... For somewhere so remote it also remarkably offers a good pub at the start, a good pub on the route itself AND a good tearoom. Fall in, fill up, flake out.

The Ride

A short climb then a long descent on wide forest tracks gives you a chance to warm up and chew the fat. After the B3357 the character of the ride changes completely. A testing descent, testing flat sections alongside the river between boulders then the first magical stepping stone crossing of the West Dart River, probably the best of all the river crossings on this ride. The Forest Inn at Hexworthy is your pub on the route or alternatively keep your appetite for Brimpts Farm Tearoom, coming soon after an interesting woodland descent and the third stepping stone crossing. You've stepped across the West Dart now step across the East Dart, climb to beyond Babeny to enjoy perhaps the finest descent of the day with views of Laughter Hole Farm ahead (now where did that name come from?). The climb up the other side is rough and loose but you are soon back on the outward route and wide forest tracks or lanes take you back to the start.

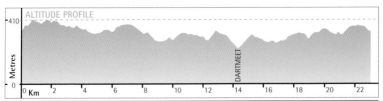

BELLEVER FOREST & THE STEPPING STONES   **GRADE:** ▲

TOTAL DISTANCE: 23KM » **TOTAL ASCENT**: 440M » **TIME**: 3–4 HOURS » **START/FINISH**: POSTBRIDGE » **START GRID REF**: SX 646789 » **SATNAV**: PL20 6TH » **PARKING**: POSTBRIDGE VISITOR CENTRE CAR PARK » **OS MAP**: EXPLORER OL28 **PUB**: FOREST INN, HEXWORTHY, TEL: 01364 631 211 » **CAFÉ**: BRIMPTS FARM TEAROOM, TEL: 01364 631 450

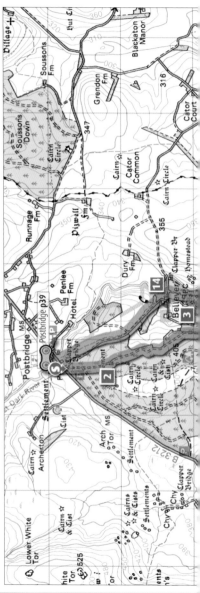

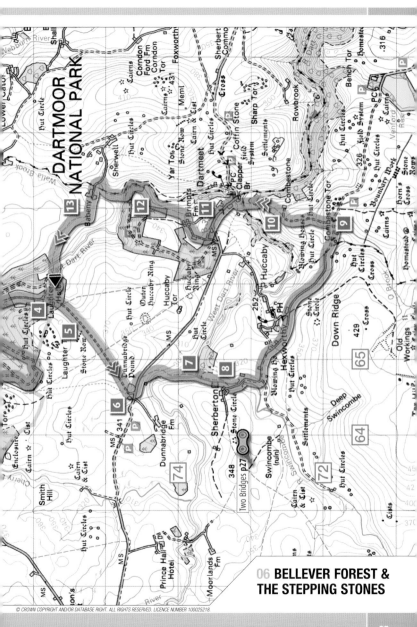

**06 BELLEVER FOREST &
THE STEPPING STONES**

➊ Exit the car park and turn **R** towards Tavistock. Take the first road **L** signposted *Youth Hostel*, turn **R** into the forest then fork **L** onto a broad forest road beyond the gate signposted *Public Footpath*.

2 Climb steadily, **ignore** a right turn near the start then after 400m take the **left-hand** track at a fork near a yellow-banded wooden post. Follow the broad forest track on a long, gentle descent for 4km.

3 At an obvious T-junction, with a bridlegate in a wire fence ahead (and beyond this, wooden picnic tables and a gravel car parking area) turn **R**, soon following signs for *Laughter Hole Farm*.

4 Go through a field gate set in a stone wall. After 400m go past a large stone barn, through another gate and bear **R** signposted *Bridlepath, County Road, Huccaby Cottage*. (The track to the left is the return route.)

5 Climb to a bridlegate in the stone wall and stay on the main **right-hand** track signposted *Dunnabridge Pound*. Fine open views. Climb then descend.

6 Go through a bridlegate and at the road (B3357) bear **L** gently uphill. **Easy to miss:** about 70m after crossing the cattlegrid bear **R** onto a narrow, unmarked track. This is at times tricky with stones (or boulders) on the descent then alongside the river.

7 Follow the main track to the point where it crosses the river via amazing 'stepping boulders' (the first of several such crossings). Follow the grassy track (at times faint) parallel with the woodland on the right. More boulder fields. Potentially boggy in winter and after heavy rain.

8 Second stepping stones crossing. Go through a gate and bear **L** onto the road. At the T-junction bear **R** uphill signposted *Holne* (or turn sharp **L** downhill for the Forest Inn in Hexworthy).

9 Cross the bridge and climb steeply. As the gradient eases, turn **L** on a broad stone track signposted *Farm Entrance* between rows of stones (there is a blue arrow on a wooden post).

10 The stone track turns to tarmac. About 100m **before** the farm turn **L** down the field edge by the wall signposted *Dartmeet*. Keep the wall to your right. Join a more obvious track and continue downhill, at times technical. Cross the river via a third set of stepping stones. Climb and turn **R** through a gate immediately beyond the house then turn **L** steeply uphill on road.

11 Turn first **R** signposted *Brimpts Farm*. Go through the farm, past the tearoom, bear **L** then **R** between buildings soon picking up *Path* signposts as you descend towards the river. Go down a wide smooth track to the field gate by a ruin. Cross the field and go through a bridlegate.

12 Tricky route between boulders alongside the river. Fourth set of stepping stones. Technical rocky challenge with the occasional carry. Cross the clapper bridge then at the tarmac turn **L**. Follow the road to the farm, turn **R** on concrete path then take the middle of the three tracks ahead (stone and earth, signposted with a blue arrow). Go through a gate and keep close to the wall to the left.

13 Climb, then technical descent with views of an amazing white house ahead. More stepping stones. Rock-strewn push uphill. At the T-junction with wide stone and gravel track turn **R**, rejoining the outward route: go through the gate, past a stone building and over open ground.

14 After 1.1km, on a sweeping left-hand bend, bear **R** through the bridlegate to go past the gravel car parking area and continue in the same direction to the road. You now have a choice:

> **OR** at the road turn **L** then **R** and return to Postbridge on tarmac.

> **OR** go **SA** onto the bridleway and follow this parallel with the lane back to the start.

⊷◖○◗ **Making a day of it**

The Postbridge & Challacombe Down ride (page 39) shares the same starting point. The Challacombe ride could in turn easily link to the Grimspound & Hound Tor ride (page 45) at Headland Warren Farm (SX 693812). At the southern end of the ride described here, there is a short overlap with the Two Bridges, Princetown & Hexworthy ride (page 27) to the south of Sherberton (SX 646733).

JOHN HORSCROFT CLIMBS ONTO HEADLAND WARREN

Introduction

This is a remarkably easy ride for its location, right in the heart of the moor: basically you never leave Dartmoor's central plateau, spending all your time between 300m and 450m. There are nevertheless some magic moments and even a bit of tricky singletrack down through heather to the tin mine ruins. And the fire never goes out in Warren House Inn...

The Ride

The gentle gradients as you make your way past Lydgate House Hotel and across the field to a better stone track have only one drawback: when it is wet you are likely to have to navigate a mudbath where the stream and the path become one! Beyond the handsome stone buildings of Pizwell Farm, an old unclassified road transports you back a hundred years to what all roads must have been like pre-tarmac. The navigation is a little bit tricky around Soussons Farm with diagonal crossings of fields and no real sign of a path until crossing the West Webburn River. The gently-climbing grassy track between ferns past the ruins of the medieval village of Challacombe leads to Warren House Farm, beyond which fern turns to heather and the track narrows. A testing section of singletrack brings you down to the ruins of Birch Tor and Vitifer tin mines and the option to climb up to the Warren House Inn. No thirst? Continue down the valley into Soussons Forest, choosing the bridlepath or forest road option to regain the road near the splendidly named Ephraim's Pinch. One last short off-road section through Lower Merripit cuts the corner to deliver you back on the B3212, a stone's throw from the start.

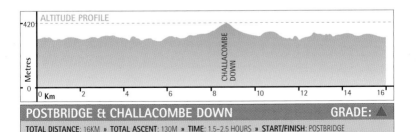

ALTITUDE PROFILE

420

Metres

CHALLACOMBE DOWN

0

0 Km   2   4   6   8   10   12   14   16

POSTBRIDGE & CHALLACOMBE DOWN   **GRADE:** ▲

TOTAL DISTANCE: 16KM » **TOTAL ASCENT**: 130M » **TIME**: 1.5-2.5 HOURS » **START/FINISH**: POSTBRIDGE
START GRID REF: SX 646789 » **SATNAV**: PL20 6TH » **PARKING**: POSTBRIDGE VISITOR CENTRE CAR PARK
OS MAP: EXPLORER OL28 » **PUB**: WARREN HOUSE INN, TEL: 01822 880 208 » **CAFÉ**: BRING SANDWICHES

07 **POSTBRIDGE & CHALLACOMBE DOWN**

➔ Exit the car park and turn **L** on the B3212. Cross the bridge and turn **R** onto the narrow lane signposted *Lydgate House, Bridlepath to Lydgate and Pizwell*. Go past the hotel and continue in the same direction on a track through a gate and into the field.

2 Follow the well-signposted grassy track alongside the river then continue on the main track as it bears **L** up and away from the river. Follow around the field edge to join a more defined earth and stone track. At one point a stream crosses the path – this is a potential mudbath.

3 Follow the wide track through Pizwell Farm and go **SA** onto the track opposite, **ignoring** the tarmac lane to the left. Cross the stream via the ford or stepping stones.

4 At the T-junction with the road turn **R** then, **easy to miss:** on gentle descent after 500m take the first **L** onto a broad stone track with a blue arrow on a wooden post.

5 Just before the farm go through the gate (by a tall wooden signpost) then turn **R** signposted *Challacombe Farm*. Follow signs along the field edge towards the wood then, before reaching the wood, go through the gate in the stone wall to the **R**. Follow the track round to the **R** and descend to cross the stream.

6 Join a better stone-based track which turns to concrete through the farm. After 50m, as the concrete drive swings right towards the road, continue **SA** through the gate signposted *Bridlepath* past a stone house. Follow this fine gentle grassy track between ferns.

7 After 1.5km, at the outbuildings, bear **L** to go through the farm and through a bridlegate. Climb to a T-junction of tracks and turn **L** signposted *Bridlepath to Warren House Inn*. Continue climbing on a narrow track.

8 Descend. At the T-junction with a broader stone path just before the ruins and the stream turn **L** towards the edge of the forest (or continue **SA** uphill for Warren House Inn). Go through the gate then shortly bear **R** at a fork of tracks signposted *Bridlepath to County Road near Soussons*. Join the forest road and turn **L**.

9   You can either follow this wide gravel forest track back to the tarmac road or use the bridlepath which starts shortly on the **R**, on a sweeping left-hand bend by a two-way signpost (SX 682799). Cross the main forest road and aim towards the gate and farm ahead to rejoin the outward route. Whichever route you choose, at the road turn **R**.

10   Cross the bridge over the stream, climb, then shortly after the summit, and immediately after crossing a cattlegrid, turn **L** downhill on the next broad stone track. Go through the gate and follow the track between buildings onto a green lane.

11   Go through Merripit Farm and take the next broad stone track to the **L**. Continue **SA** then at the T-junction with the B3212 turn **L** to return to start.

⊶⊙⊙ Making a day of it

The Bellever & the Stepping Stones ride (page 33) also starts from Postbridge. Also, at the north-eastern end of the ride at Headland Warren Farm you are very close to the Grimspound & Hound Tor ride (page 45) at SX 697808.

HOUND TOR

Introduction

This is the toughest of all the Dartmoor rides and probably the most scenic, with little by way of rough, bleak featureless moorland and lots by way of dramatic tors, dingly dells, big granite farmhouses, killer climbs and fast descents.

The Ride

Start by plunging down into the wooded valley formed by the River Bovey then climb steeply back out of it up to Water. A gentler interlude follows on easier tracks past quaint Dartmoor houses, through Manaton, along minor lanes and on a wide stone track below Easdon Tor with fine views of the route ahead on Hameldown. Take time to look at the size of the stones in the walls of West Coombe – how did they move those without JCBs? Are you ready for the climb? 130m in little over a kilometre with a very steep concrete track at the start. Lose some of your precious height on tarmac before climbing past the

Bronze Age settlement at Grimspound and a wonderful open grassy descent with vast views ahead. It is at this point that me and the lads tend to break out into a burst of 'The Magnificent Seven'. Further on, Jay's Grave always has fresh wildflowers laid on it. Even in winter. By whom? One of those still-waters-run-deep mysteries. Hound Tor is spectacular, no doubt about it. If you are in luck you can refuel at the tea wagon, called, wait for it 'Hound of the Basket Meals'! If you are looking for technical challenges, fill your boots with them over the next kilometre by trying to ride as much as possible of the pixieland landscape east of Hound Tor towards Leighon. The show is almost over but there is one last firework – climb to the road above Yarner Wood then glide down the superb track on its southern edge, briefly touching the road before a second, narrower bridleway brings you back to the start.

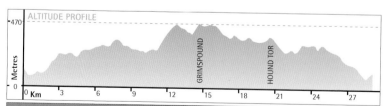

ALTITUDE PROFILE

470

Metres

0 Km   3   6   9   12   15   18   21   24   27

GRIMSPOUND   HOUND TOR

GRIMSPOUND & HOUND TOR   GRADE: ▲

TOTAL DISTANCE: 29KM » **TOTAL ASCENT**: 690M » **TIME**: 4-5 HOURS » **START/FINISH**: TRENDLEBERE DOWN, WEST OF BOVEY TRACEY ON THE ROAD TOWARDS MANATON » **START GRID REF**: SX 785794 » **SATNAV**: LUSTLEIGH (CLOSEST) » **PARKING**: TRENDLEBERE DOWN CAR PARK » **OS MAP**: EXPLORER OL28 » **PUB**: KESTOR INN, MANATON, TEL: 01647 221 626 » **CAFÉ**: OFTEN A TEA WAGON IN THE HOUND TOR CAR PARK

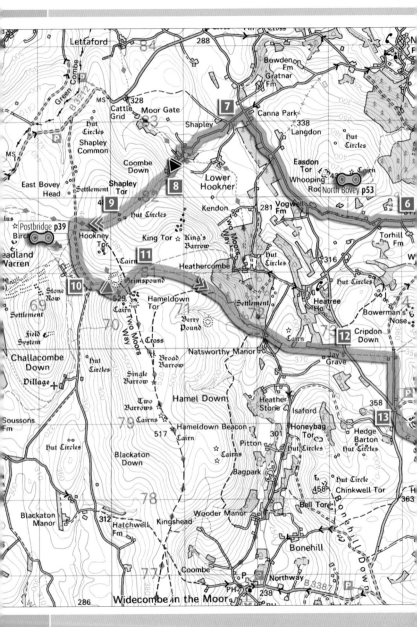

08 GRIMSPOUND & HOUND TOR

6 Turn **L** downhill out of the car park then shortly **L** again, sharply back on yourself signposted *Unsuitable for Motors*. Go downhill then along the (muddy) stone track along the valley bottom for 1.7km.

2 **Ignore** the first bridge/gate to the right. Cross Becka Brook via the second stone bridge (SX 773803) by a two-way *Path* sign. The trail zigzags up through the forestry. Steep climb.

3 At a crossroads of tracks continue **SA** uphill signposted *Bridlepath to Water for Manaton*. Join tarmac as the gradient eases. At a Y-shaped junction turn **R** signposted *Bridlepath to Bovey Valley for Lustleigh and Manaton (indirect)*. Go past a thatched house (Endacott) and shortly turn **L** just before the next house signposted *Bridlepath*.

4 At a crossroads of tracks turn **L** (there is a private drive to the right), following signs for Manaton, then at the next junction of tracks by a small corrugated iron shed turn **L** uphill signposted *Bridlepath to Manaton*.

5 Attractive singletrack with some roots and rocks. At the T-junction with the road turn **L**. Big stones in the wall ahead. At the crossroads turn **R** signposted *Hound Tor, Widecombe*. Busier road.

6 After 1.2km **ignore** the first road right at Langstone Cross. After 500m take the next **R** onto a no through road signposted *Barracott*. The tarmac turns to track signposted *Byway*. Climb then descend. At the T-junction with the road turn **R**.

7 After 1.6km, on a gentle descent, at a crossroads of minor lanes (your priority) turn **L** downhill onto a no through road signposted *Hookner Coombe*. **Ignore** turns to the left then right.

8 Go past a house with fridge-size stones. Exceedingly steep climb on concrete and grass track. As the track swings right towards the house bear **L** to continue in same direction uphill, signposted *Bridleway*.

9 The stone track turns to grass through ferns. Long steep climb with ever better views behind. Turn **R** through a gate in the wall then turn **L** to continue in same direction, soon reaching the top. Drop down to the road and turn **L**.

10 **Easy to miss:** descend on tarmac for 700m, keeping your brakes on, then about 50m **before** the start of a sweeping right-hand bend, and opposite a passing place on the right, keep an eye out for a grassy track bearing **L** up and away from the road. Climb towards then around the stone ruins of Grimspound (keep the wall to your left).

11 Climb for 1.2km to the summit – excellent panoramic views over rolling Devon patchwork of fields and clumps of woodland with tors on the horizon to the right. Follow towards the **right-hand** end of forest. Superb descent. At the T-junction with the road turn **L** then **R** signposted *Bridlepath to Jay's Grave*.

12 At the road by Jay's Grave go **SA** uphill through a gate ahead onto a wide grassy track signposted *Bridleway*. Go round the edge of the field through a bridlegate and continue **SA** downhill (i.e. **not** right on a more obvious track towards the barn). At the road turn **R**.

13 At the road junction with a thatched house ahead bear **L** then shortly, at the point where a road joins from the left (tea wagon in car park), go **SA** onto grass towards the right-hand end of Hound Tor (there is a blue arrow on wooden post).

14 Climb past Hound Tor and aim downhill towards the left-hand end of Greator Rocks ahead, where rocks meet woodland. Go through the bridlegate just to the **R** of a stack of rocks signposted *Bridlepath to Leighon via Haytor Down*. Testing narrow descent with stone drainage channels. Cross a stone bridge over the stream.

15 Much of next 1.2km is a walk through dingly dell boulder fields. Emerge at a wooden post and bear **L** signposted *Bridlepath to Leighon*. Go through several gates and follow the track as it turns sharp **R** uphill signposted *County Road below Blackhill*. Steep push then the track levels out for superb views.

16 At the T-junction with the road turn **R** gently uphill. After 800m ignore a bridlepath to the left just after the start of the wood then ignore a second left (East Dartmoor Nature Reserve). Continue climbing, then, as the gradient eases, keep an eye out for a signpost set back from the road *Bridlepath to Haytor Bovey Road near Ullacombe* pointing alongside the wall, bearing **L** away from the road (SX 769783). Superb descent though woodland.

17 At the T-junction with road turn **L**, then **easy to miss:** on a fast descent take the **fourth L** – the first three are tarmac (drives), the fourth is a wide, level gravel track signposted *Bridlepath to Manaton Road at Reddaford Water.*

18 At crossroads of tracks with Templer Way continue **SA** downhill. At the bottom of this track, at the T-junction with the road, turn **L** for 800m, climbing to return to the car park at the start (just after the cattle grid).

◄◦◦◦◦ Making a day of it

To the north this can easily link to the North Bovey & Foxworthy ride (page 53) as it shares about 1km of lanes and tracks either side of Easdon Farm (SX 728818). To the west, a short bridleway link from the road below Hookney Tor brings you to Headland Warren Farm and the Postbridge & Challacombe Down ride (page 39). Seekers of Super-Tech™ should check out the Nut Crackers trail near Lustleigh too – just how much of it can you ride?

THE GIANT'S CHAIR, NEAR JAY'S GRAVE PHOTO: TIM RUSSON

PHOTO: TIM RUSSON

09 North Bovey, Whooping Rock & Foxworthy

14km

Introduction

This is the little brother ride to the mighty Grimspound & Hound Tor ride (p45). It has the same east edge of Dartmoor feel with fine views towards Hameldown and the same mix of handsome granite houses, thatched roofs, stone walls and narrow lanes. North Bovey is a picture postcard village and has a decent pub for your return. If you like the appetiser, try the main course next!

The Ride

Bish bash bosh, cross the River Bovey and climb 145m, just like that. About half is on tarmac then half on a good stone-based track, suddenly offering huge views ahead of King Tor, Shapley Tor and Hameldown Tor. The ride skirts the flanks of Easdon Tor, using a lane on the west side then you are back onto a track climbing towards the summit before contouring around to a very easily missed path leading down into the conifer plantation. Swoosh down through the trees, ease up a little for the singletrack to get you down to the road. Keep losing height to cross the River Bovey at the pretty little hamlet of Foxworthy before climbing back up on track and lane to Barnecourt. Decisions, decisions: is it hot enough, or is your bike muddy enough, for you to go for a splash in the ford just before reaching North Bovey, or do you play it safe and arrive dry for the pub?

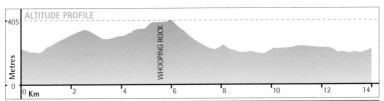

ALTITUDE PROFILE

405

Metres

0

WHOOPING ROCK

0 Km   2   4   6   8   10   12   14

NORTH BOVEY, WHOOPING ROCK & FOXWORTHY **GRADE:** ▲

TOTAL DISTANCE: 14KM » **TOTAL ASCENT:** 250M » **TIME:** 1.5–2.5 HOURS » **START/FINISH:** NORTH BOVEY
START GRID REF: SX 741838 » **SATNAV:** TQ13 8RB » **PARKING:** NORTH BOVEY CAR PARK OPPOSITE THE CHURCH
OS MAP: EXPLORER OL28 » **PUB:** RING OF BELLS, NORTH BOVEY, TEL: 01647 440 375 » **CAFÉ:** BRING SANDWICHES

PHOTO: TIM RUSSON

09 **NORTH BOVEY, WHOOPING ROCK & FOXWORTHY**

Directions – North Bovey, Whooping Rock & Foxworthy

➲ Turn **L** out of North Bovey car park, first **R** at Fairbrook Bridge then at the T-junction turn **L** signposted *Manaton*. Steep climb. Ignore a right turn at Yarde Cross to Moreton-hampstead then, **easy to miss**, after 400m keep an eye out for a wide stone track climbing to the **L** signposted *Byway to Langdon and Bridlepath to Easdon*. Fine views across the valley to Hameldown.

2 At the junction with tarmac by a farm turn **L**. Steep descent. At the T-junction with the road turn **L** then after almost 1km take the first road **L** by *Easdon* signs. The tarmac turns to track by a cluster of buildings signposted *Byway to Barracott*. Go through a gate, still climbing.

3 Just before the next gate, at the top of the climb, turn **L** uphill signposted *Bridlepath to County Road near Luckdon via Easdon* (the sign is tucked into the hedge to the right). The track leads towards the tor then bears **R** to run parallel with the wall to your right.

4 At the corner of the wall **DO NOT** go straight ahead but turn **R** and follow a faint track as it contours around the hillside through fern and gorse. At the **next** wall corner continue **SA** towards the conifer plantation ahead.

5 **Easy to miss:** after 150m, shortly after a large flat boulder on the right, bear **R** downhill through ferns on faint track. Go through a bridlegate into the woodland onto a grass then stone track.

6 Again, **easy to miss:** fast descent for 1km, then on sweeping left-hand bend keep an eye out for a **R** turn to continue downhill on a grassy track. This is just before a two-way *Path* sign on the left. There is also a *Bridleway* sign for the right turn but it is hidden in the ferns!

7 Descend, bear **L** to go through a gate and continue downhill. Go through a gate onto the road, turn **R**, climb, then take the first road on the **L** by Langstone Cottage signposted *Lustleigh*. **Easy to miss:** (keep your brakes on) after 400m on this fast descent turn first road **R** signposted *Manaton, Unsuitable for wide vehicles*.

8 Descend then climb. On a sharp right-hand bend bear **L** (in effect go **SA**) signposted *Bridlepath to Foxworthy Bridge*. At the bottom of the descent on a concrete and grass track, just before a gate and a *Private* sign, turn **R** onto a narrow track signposted *Path*. Rejoin the concrete track and turn **R**.

9 Shortly fork **L** signposted *Bridlepath for Peck Farm and road near Barnecourt* and go past a large thatched house. Follow blue arrows through the right-hand gate. Climb on a narrow, walled track, go through the gate and turn **L** onto a concrete track.

10 At the T-junction with the road turn **R** then shortly after the brow of the hill turn **L** just before the buildings onto a no through road alongside a long stone wall. The tarmac turns to track.

11 At a signpost for *North Bovey Village* you have a choice – turn **L** for the ford/stepping stones signposted *Byway to Manaton Road* then turn **R** to return to the car park OR go **SA** into the village, and keep bearing **L** to return to same point. Do you want to wash your bike?

◄◎◎ Making a day of it

This is tailor-made to be linked to the Grimspound & Hound Tor ride (page 45) for a longer day out. Do the following: start from North Bovey, follow this ride to the road just after Langdon (SX 724827), turn **R** to join the Grimspound ride through West Coombe and over Hookney Tor. On the return, at the road in Manaton, turn **R** at SX 751814 to pick up the North Bovey ride near to Foxworthy at SX 753823.

PHOTO: TIM RUSSON

PUBLIC BRIDLEPATH
ROAD NEAR
FIRTH BRIDGE 1¼ M

P
MANA
&

PHOTO: TIM RUSSON

10 Avon Dam & Scorriton

27km

Introduction

This is one of the longest and toughest rides featured, although it rarely feels as remote as other rides as it hugs the southeast corner of the National Park. South Brent certainly doesn't feel like a Dartmoor village and it is only up towards the Avon Dam Reservoir where you sense a degree of remoteness. But if you like fast open descents this ride has them in buckets.

The Ride

The southern and southeastern fringes of Dartmoor are characterised by patchworks of small fields and a lane network that heads up towards the moor then turns back as though it is too daunting to venture any further in. North of South Brent the lanes and tracks are followed to their edge-of-the-moor limit at Shipley Bridge before joining the service road/track that leads to Avon Dam Reservoir. A brief rough section on the Abbots Way to the highpoint of the ride at 390m leads to a stream crossing then a fine, fast open grassy descent down to a collection of big rooty trees, full of character by the ford of Dean Burn. A second (optional) loop once again heads on the lane network towards the moor at Lud Gate, before a second ford, a short climb then a long fast descent down to Scorriton and the chance of a beer. The crossing of the River Mardle just south of Scorriton is at 117m. An unforgiving lane climb then a broad stone track takes you up to 340m with wonderful views east, setting you up for the final grassy off-road descent, though not the final road descent. What has gone up must come down and there's still plenty to go for the lane zoom through Lutton back to the delights of South Brent.

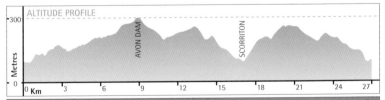

ALTITUDE PROFILE

300

Metres

0

0 Km   3   6   9   12   15   18   21   24   27

AVON DAM

SCORRITON

AVON DAM & SCORRITON

GRADE: ▲

TOTAL DISTANCE: 27KM » **TOTAL ASCENT**: 700M » **TIME**: 3-4 HOURS » **START/FINISH**: SOUTH BRENT, OFF THE A38 WEST OF TOTNES » **START GRID REF**: SX 697603 » **SATNAV**: SOUTH BRENT » **PARKING**: CAR PARK BY THE RAILWAY LINE, JUST OFF MAIN STREET IN SOUTH BRENT » **OS MAP**: EXPLORER OL28 » **PUB**: TRADESMAN'S ARMS, SCORRITON, TEL: 01364 631 206 » **CAFÉ**: LOTS OF CHOICE IN SOUTH BRENT

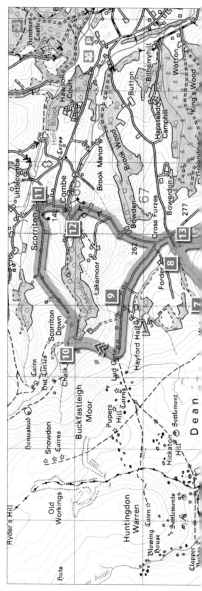

10 AVON DAM & SCORRITON

➊ Turn **R** out of South Brent car park. At the T-junction turn **R**, cross the railway bridge then bear **L** (in effect **SA**) signposted *2 ton weight limit*. After 400m take the first road **R** signposted *Lutton*.

2 Climb steeply then steadily, ignoring a road to the right. After almost 800m, turn **L** downhill onto a lane by a triangle of grass and a road grit bin, shortly bearing **R** onto a broad stone track signposted *Bridlepath to Didworthy*.

3 Cross the ford, go through several gates, climb steeply then steadily as the track narrows, passing through two bridlegates. This section may be overgrown. Climb to the summit, shortly go through a third gate then at the tarmac by houses continue **SA** downhill, following the road around a sharp left-hand bend.

4 At the T-junction with a barn ahead turn **L** downhill, cross the river then at the next T-junction turn **R** signposted *Shipley Bridge* onto a no through road. Immediately after the car park but **before** the bridge turn **L** onto a tarmac lane signposted *Brockhill Ford (Abbots Way)*.

5 After 1.2km cross the stream, leave the woodland and emerge onto open moorland. About 1.2km after the stream crossing, on a sweeping left-hand bend, bear **R** uphill onto a broad gravel track climbing away from the road up to the dam.

6 The track is rougher after the dam. At the first 'corner' of the reservoir bear **R** away from the water then after 400m of testing stone-strewn track, at the junction with a wider, more defined grassy track coming from the left, turn **R** steeply uphill on an eroded grass track (this is Abbots Way). Pass to the **L** of a small plantation and go through a bridlegate signposted *Abbots Way*.

7 Descend to cross the stream. Short steep climb then immediately fork **L** on lower path (blue arrow). **Easy to miss:** following blue-topped posts on a fast grassy descent, bear **L** through a bridlegate in the fence to the left down into woodland.

8 Go through two gates by Lord of the Rings beech trees and roots. Follow a signpost for *Cross Furzes**. Cross the stream via the clapper bridge or the ford. Steep broad, stony climb.

> ◢OR◣ *For a shortcut, turn **R** signposted *Moor Cross, South Brent.*

At the crossroads with tarmac at the top turn **L** signposted *Combe, Scorriton, Hayford Hall*. After 400m fork **L** signposted *Hayford Hall.*

9 At the end of the tarmac go **SA** onto a wide stone track. Go through the gate onto the moor signposted *Bridlepath to Scorriton via Chalk Ford* and shortly fork **R** towards the wall/fence corner to your right (i.e. do **not** take the more obvious track ahead up onto the moor). Soon cross the stream.

10 **Ignore** the first narrow grassy track to the right alongside the wall but after this aim to bear **R** and descend steeply into the valley to your right on a grass and stone track, to arrive at a narrow wooden bridge over the stream. After a short climb this becomes a long fast descent on a broad, loose stone track.

11 Join tarmac then at the T-junction in Scorriton turn **R** (*or turn **L** for Tradesman's Arms pub*). Shortly, on a sharp left-hand bend turn **R** signposted *Lower Coombe, Higher Coombe.*

12 Descend, cross the stream and climb, ignoring turns to left and right. Long, steep tarmac climb. Rejoin the outward route at Cross Furzes. **Ignore** a right turn to Hayford Hall then, opposite a road to the left to Buckfast, turn **R** downhill on a broad stone track.

13 Steep descent, cross the stream, turn **L** signposted *Bridlepath to Moor Cross for South Brent*. Steep then steady climb to emerge on the moor. Follow this grassy track running parallel with a wall to the left with fantastic views.

Directions – Avon Dam & Scorriton
continued...

14 Continue in the same direction, passing through two closely spaced gates with blue paint splashes. Almost immediately turn **R** through a field gate and go down across the field bearing slightly away from the fence on the left to aim for a gate and signpost in the fence ahead at the bottom of the field.

15 Follow the direction of the signpost diagonally **R** across the field to the far corner to find a hidden bridlegate. Go through the gate and turn **L**. Emerge at the road, bear **R** then take the first road **R** by a triangle of grass.

16 Final climb. At the T-junction at the top by Bloody Pool Cross turn **R** signposted *Shipley Bridge* then shortly **L** signposted *Lutton*. Fast descent. At the T-junction at the bottom turn **L** to return to South Brent.

⊶◯◯ Making a day of it

It's about 5km northwest from Scorriton via Venford Reservoir to link with the Bellever & the Stepping Stones ride (page 33) at SX 668719 (south of Dartmeet). Alternatively, thinking out of the box, you could use the very steep, very beautiful lanes to go north to the great little village of Widecombe in the Moor to visit Uncle Tom Cobley.

SECTION 2

Exmoor

Square mile for square mile, Exmoor is surely the best National Park in the UK for mountain biking - can anywhere else boast such quantity, quality and variety of trails? Routes up on the cliff tops with views across the Bristol Channel to Wales; intimate wooded combes with twisting, testing rooty singletrack; remote moorland that could easily be compared to that in the Peak District or further north; and then there is the speciality of the region - rollercoaster bedrock descents with enough drop-offs to test the keenest mountain biker. There really is something on Exmoor to suit every rider.

APPROACHING COUNTY GATE ON THE SOUTHWEST COAST PATH (ROUTE 13)

THE CLIMB FROM ROBBER'S BRIDGE (ROUTE 13)

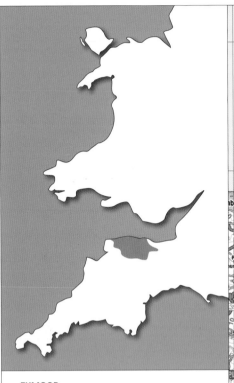

EXMOOR

BRISTOL CHANNEL

Foreland Point
Countisbury
South West Coast Path
Porlock Bay
Bossington
Selworthy Beacon
North Hill
MINEHEAD
Culbone Toll
Hill Porlock Weir
West Porlock
Porlock
Allerford
Selworthy
West Luccombe
Blue Anchor Bay
B3191
WATC
Brendon
Oare
13
A39
Luccombe
Alcombe
Dunster
Blue Anchor
Old
Cleeve
Castle
12
Brendon
Common
14
Wootton
Courtenay
Timberscombe
A396
Carhampton
Withycombe
Bilbrook
Washford
Rodhuish
Abbey
Sampford
Brett
Ve
15
Dunkery Hill
519
EXMOOR
NATIONAL PARK
435
FOREST
River Exe
Simonsbath
Exford
B3224
Luckwell
Bridge
Cutcombe
Wheddon
Cross
Lype Hill
Luxborough
Crow
Hill
21
Roadwater
Monksilver
Stog
Combe
Sydenham
22
Elworthy
B3224
EXMOOR
Long
Holcombe
River Barle
391
17
Wi
Common
Withypool
Winsford
19
B3224
BRENDON HILLS
411
Treborough
290
B3190
Brompton
Ralph
Pitsfo
North
Radworthy
South
Radworthy
428
Winsford
Hill
428
Liscombe
Tarr Steps
Exton
Bridgetown
Withiel
Florey
Brompton
Regis
Wimbleball
Lake
Clatworthy
Reservoir
Clatworthy
La
Me
16
18
Twitchen
Molland
Common
Hawkridge
River Barle
20
317
Upton
Huish
Champflower
Maundown
338
Wivelliscomb
Molland
West
Anstey
East
Anstey
Dulverton
355
Bury
Skilgate
Chipstable
Waterrow
West
Yeo Mill
Battleton
Brushford
Oldways
End
268
247
Morebath
Petton
B3227
Clayhanger
Ash Mill
arunsleigh
Knowstone
Roachill
B3227
Oakfordbridge
Exebridge
240
Shillingford
Bampton
Be
267
Rose Ash
16
Oakford
Meshaw
238
Creacombe
Stoodleigh
Beacon
301
Stoodle

**EXMOOR AREA MAP
& ROUTE FINDER**

CONTAINS ORDNANCE SURVEY DATA © CROWN COPYRIGHT AND DATABASE RIGHT

LEAVING LYNTON AND THE VALLEY OF ROCKS

11 Lynton & the Valley of Rocks

22km

Introduction

This ride would be worth it for the sea views alone. Throw in the Valley of Rocks, a wonderfully graded zigzag climb up through woods from Lee Abbey and some great stream crossings in hidden combes and you have a fine coast and moors ride. And then there is the descent down to Lyn Bridge.

The Ride

Lynton is the biggest town on Exmoor and is a real tourist hub. Tear yourself away from the postcard shops and cream teas and enjoy the easy warm-up on tarmac through the spectacular Valley of Rocks, one of the few places on Exmoor where you can go rock climbing. A fine graded (bike) climb with great sea views takes you up to the edge of the moorland, first on track then on quiet lanes. The descents and climbs to cross the valleys cut by the streams running down off the moor seem to get steeper and steeper: Barbrook is followed by the West Lyn River then Hoaroak River (twice) before the final long climb sets you up at West Lyn Farmhouse for the best downhill of the day down to Lyn Bridge. Still in one piece? Enjoy your rewards among the bright lights of Lynton.

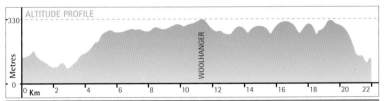

ALTITUDE PROFILE

330

WOOLHANGER

Metres

0

0 Km 2 4 6 8 10 12 14 16 18 20 22

LYNTON & THE VALLEY OF ROCKS   GRADE: ▲

TOTAL DISTANCE: 22KM » **TOTAL ASCENT**: 400M » **TIME**: 2.5–3.5 HOURS » **START/FINISH**: LYNTON
START GRID REF: SS 720494 » **SATNAV**: LYNTON » **PARKING**: BOTTOM MEADOW CAR PARK AT THE EAST END OF LYNTON » **OS MAP**: EXPLORER OL9 » **PUB**: LOTS OF CHOICE IN LYNTON » **CAFÉ**: LOTS OF CHOICE IN LYNTON

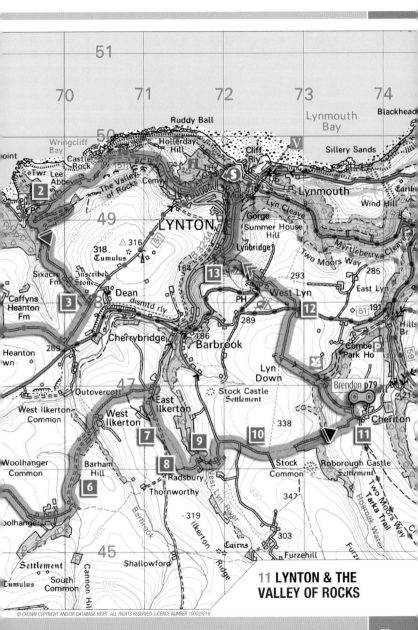

11 LYNTON & THE VALLEY OF ROCKS

5▸ Exit Bottom Meadow car park and turn **L** uphill following the main road through Lynton for almost 3km, past the shops then towards and through the Valley of Rocks.

2 Shortly after the start of the Lee Abbey buildings on your right, opposite the gate tower, bear **L** through a gate onto a broad stone track signposted *Bridleway to Six Acre Cross*. Fabulous sea cliff views. After 400m turn **L** sharply back on yourself - same sign, there is a footpath ahead. Superb climbing track. Another zigzag, all well signposted.

3 Go through two bridlegates by the farm onto tarmac. At the T-junction with the road at the end of the farm drive, turn **R** (by a caravan park). At the next T-junction (with a letter box in the hedgerow ahead) turn **R** signposted *National Cycle Network Route 51*.

4 After 2.5km at a crossroads of lanes (Martinhoe Common Cross) take the first road **L** signposted *Parracombe*. At the offset crossroads with the A39 at Martinhoe Cross turn **L** then **R** onto a no through road signposted *Woolhanger*.

5 **Ignore** a road to the right. Tarmac turns to track. At fork bear **L** signposted *Woolhanger Estate Office*. Go downhill past buildings, round a sharp left-hand bend then shortly bear **L** at fork near to an isolated house and follow round to the **L** signposted *Permitted Bridleway to West Ilkerton*.

6 Descend on concrete then stone track. Cross a small river then climb steeply. At West Ilkerton Farm turn **L** on tarmac to continue climbing. At the T-junction with Manor Farm ahead turn **R**.

7 Climb steeply then more gently. Cross the cattle grid and immediately bear **L** onto a grass track running alongside the wall to the left signposted *Bridleway to Radsbury*. Grass track turns to stone track.

8 After 750m at a crossroads of tracks by a wooden post to your right (this may be partially obscured) turn **L** downhill through a gate onto a smooth, wide track signposted *Sparhanger Cross via South Sparhanger*. At the tarmac bear **L** downhill (Radsbury is to the right).

9 Descend steeply, cross the concrete-bottomed ford then climb steeply through the farm, past stables. At the T-junction turn **R** (SS 719463). Shortly, on a sharp right-hand bend, bear **L** through gate gently uphill on broad stone track signposted *Bridleway to Cheriton.*

10 At a gate go **SA** across the field (same sign), **ignoring** a wide bridleway to the right. This soon becomes an obvious track. At the end of the field follow a loose stone track down to a ford/bridge. Very steep, stony climb.

11 At the T-junction with tarmac turn **L** signposted *Lynmouth, Two Moors Way (MW).* Steep descent on what used to be a tarmac road. Climb steeply.

12 At the crossroads with the A39 go **SA** signposted *West Lyn.* Views to Wales ahead. After 650m, on a sharp left-hand bend by cluster of buildings near West Lyn Farmhouse, turn **R** then **L** between the wall and the barn signposted *Lynbridge.* Go through gate onto a sunken track between hedgerows.

13 Great descent! At the T-junction at the bottom turn **L** then **R** to cross the footbridge and emerge by the Bridge Inn. Bear **R** by the pub then turn **R** downhill on the road and continue **SA** signposted *Lynton, Valley of Rocks* to return to the car park at the start.

◄☞ **Making a day of it**

When you reach Cheriton (SS 737466) you are less than 1km southwest of the Brendon & the Doone Valley ride (page 79) at Keeper's Gate.

12 Brendon Common, the Doone Valley & the East Lyn River

21km

Introduction

Linking the beautiful wooded valley of the East Lyn River with the remote moorland of Brendon Common and the popular trail along Badgworthy Water (or Doone Country as the tourist board would have it) this ride shows once again the fantastic variety of tracks and paths that Exmoor offers.

The Ride

Just a few turns of the pedals take you from the busy A39, the main road along the north coast of Somerset and Devon, away from traffic and tourists into the maze of lanes and tracks above Farley Water. How much of the woodland zigzags can you manage? It's hello to cars again for a brief spell on the B3223 before the highest and most remote part of the ride on Brendon Common, climbing to over 400m. Just when things start getting a bit peaty and tussocky the track improves as you plunge down into the valley of Badgworthy Water. There are plenty of testing sections along here as you head north to Malmsmead and the chance of coffee and buns at The Buttery. A lung-busting climb through Southern Wood follows, once again with potential foodie rewards in Leeford, Brendon and Rockford. The ride finishes with a breathtaking balcony route through stunning broadleaf woodland high above the East Lyn River that ends right back at the car park at Hillsford Bridge.

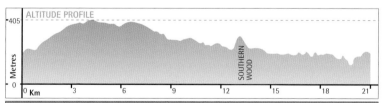

ALTITUDE PROFILE

405 — Metres — 0

0 Km   3   6   9   12   15   18   21

SOUTHERN WOOD

BRENDON COMMON & THE EAST LYN RIVER   **GRADE:** ▲

TOTAL DISTANCE: 21KM » **TOTAL ASCENT**: 450M » **TIME**: 2.5–3.5 HOURS » **START/FINISH**: A39/B3223 JUNCTION AT HILLSFORD BRIDGE, SOUTHEAST OF LYNTON » **START GRID REF**: SS 741477 » **SATNAV**: BARBROOK (CLOSEST) **PARKING**: CAR PARK AT HILLSFORD BRIDGE » **OS MAP**: EXPLORER OL9 » **PUB**: STAGHUNTERS INN, LEEFORD, TEL: 01598 741 222; ROCKFORD INN, ROCKFORD, TEL: 01598 741 214 » **CAFÉ**: THE BUTTERY, MALMSMEAD, TEL: 01598 741 106; BRENDON HOUSE TEA GARDEN, LEEFORD, TEL: 01598 741 206

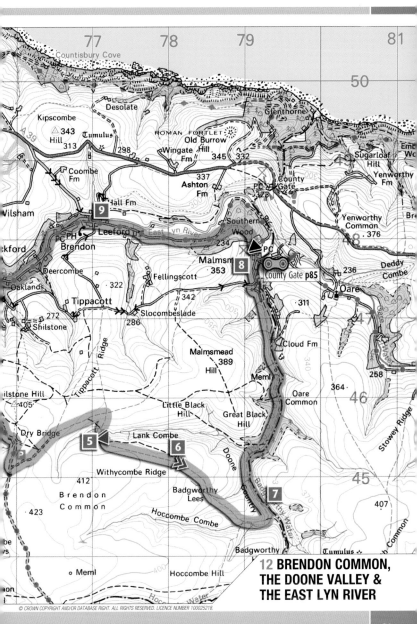

**12 BRENDON COMMON,
THE DOONE VALLEY &
THE EAST LYN RIVER**

Directions – Brendon Common, the Doone Valley & the East Lyn River

➡ Exit the Hillsford Bridge car park and turn **R** signposted *Bridge Ball, Cheriton*. After 800m follow the road downhill round a sharp left-hand bend ignoring a right turn to Cheriton. About 100m after starting to climb, turn **R** through gate into woodland signposted *Bridleway to Brendon Common*.

2 The path zigzags up through the woodland on several switchbacks. At the T-junction with the road (SS 745465) turn **R** signposted *Brendon Common* then shortly on a right-hand bend turn **L** (same sign) through a gate onto an earth and stone track.

3 Go through a second gate then, at a third gate by a 2-way signpost, stay to the **L** of the concrete post and wire fence. At the end of the field bear **R** through a gate in a stony dip then climb signposted *Bridleway to Brendon Common*.

4 Climb to the road and turn **R** gently uphill. **Ignore** a footpath to Shilstone. Continue climbing and turn **L** at the next signpost *Bridleway to Malmsmead and Brendon*.

5 After 1.5km at a 4-way post, turn **R** signposted *Doone Way*. Short, steep descent then short, steep climb. Stone track turns to rough grass.

6 Go through a gate and the track becomes less rough. At a fork after 1km bear **L** on the upper track (blue waymark) through a gap in the stone wall. After 450m at the next fork by a low square wooden post, bear **L** again on the upper track signposted *Bridleway to Malmsmead*.

7 Follow this excellent trail for 3.6km on a variety of surfaces. **Ignore** a right turn over the footbridge to Cloud Farm. Continue on the west side of Badgworthy Water.

8 At the T-junction with the road turn **R**. After 300m, opposite the shop in Malmsmead and next to a metal barn, turn **L** through a gate onto a steep stony track signposted *Bridleway to Southern Wood*. Gradient steepens. Climb to summit then descend to road and turn **L**.

9 After 1.7km at crossroads in Leeford by Brendon House Tea Garden go **SA** (your priority) signposted *Simonsbath, Barnstaple*. Go past the Staghunters Inn.

10 After 1.5km go past the Rockford Inn. Shortly, at the top of a steep climb as the gradient eases and just before a *25% climb* road sign, turn **R** through a bridlegate signposted *Hillsford Bridge*.

11 Go through a second gate and at a fork by a 3-way signpost bear **L** on the upper track signposted *Bridleway* (the lower, right-hand track is a footpath). Amazing balcony path with steep wooded hillside opposite. After 1.2km at a T-junction turn **L** signposted *Bridleway to Hillsford Bridge & Watersmeet*. At the next fork bear **L** on the upper track (same sign). Climb. At the T-junction with the road turn **R** then **L** to return to the car park at the start.

◀◉◯ Making a day of it
The start of the ride is about 1km from the Lynton & the Valley of Rocks ride (page 73) at Cheriton (SS 737466). At the eastern end, in Malmsmead, you are very close to the Porlock Weir & County Gate ride (page 85).

13 Porlock Weir & County Gate   22km

Introduction

The 500-mile Southwest Coast Path has surprisingly few sections where you can ride so make the most of this ride up above Culbone Wood with great views out over Porlock Bay and the Bristol Channel to Wales. As it starts at sea level (at a good pub) and climbs to over 400m you can look forward to a long, well-deserved descent in the final part of the ride with a beer at the end.

The Ride

Decisions, decisions! Almost as soon as the ride starts you have one to make: are you man/woman enough to climb 200m off-road on a steep bridleway or do you stick to that ever so quiet and beautiful lane running parallel, the old toll road? Both link up after 1.5km and more tiny lanes take you to a cruising height of 300m as you follow contouring tracks west past farms, through woodland and across fields with fine sea views to the excellent little visitor centre and café at County Gate (there's a beautifully crafted relief model of the area so you can see where you've been). Plummet to the bottom of the valley, via a steep grassy descent which can be slippery when wet (hey, maybe I'll write a song about that), where gates numberless to man bring you to the lane that runs up the Oare Valley and a great climb up to the Culbone Inn through pheasant city. You are almost there – at the top of the ride at 408m and Porlock Weir is only 5km away. That means down, down, down and more decisions: which off-road descent? You have three to choose from. Maybe you'll just have to come back and do them all.

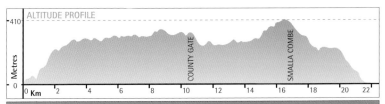

ALTITUDE PROFILE

PORLOCK WEIR & COUNTY GATE   GRADE: ▲

TOTAL DISTANCE: 22KM » **TOTAL ASCENT**: 475M » **TIME**: 2.5–3.5 HOURS » **START/FINISH**: PORLOCK WEIR, WEST OF PORLOCK » **START GRID REF**: SS 864478 » **SATNAV**: TA24 8PB » **PARKING**: PORLOCK WEIR CAR PARK, OPPOSITE THE SHIP INN » **OS MAP**: EXPLORER OL9 » **PUB**: CULBONE INN, ON THE A39 AT CULBONE HILL, TEL: 01643 862 259 **CAFÉ**: COUNTY GATE VISITOR CENTRE CAFÉ, TEL: 01598 741 321; THE BUTTERY TEAROOM, MALMSMEAD (JUST OFF ROUTE), TEL: 01598 741 202

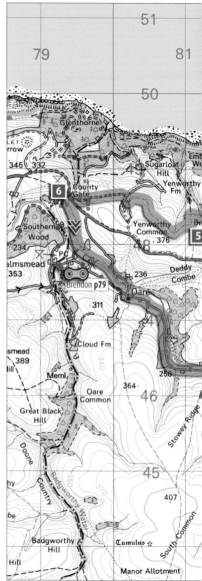

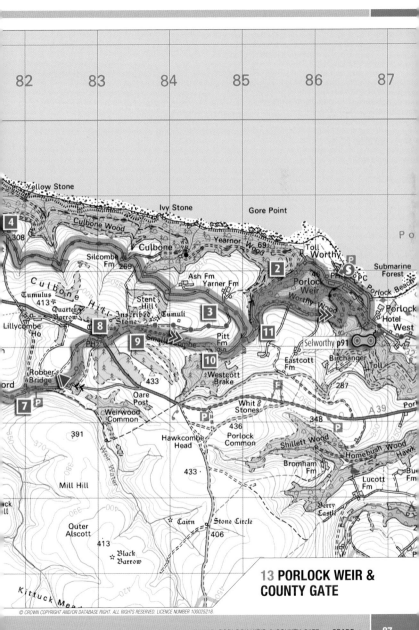

13 PORLOCK WEIR & COUNTY GATE

⮕ From the main car park in Porlock Weir cross the road onto the minor lane between the Ship Inn and Andrews on the Weir Restaurant. Short steep climb then at the T-junction turn **R** signposted *Worthy, Ashley Combe*. **Ignore** the first bridleway to the left (to Yearnor) after 200m. After a further 550m take the next track **L*** signposted *Bridleway to Worthy Combe, No Vehicles*.

> **OR** * For an alternative, easier climb on a very quiet lane, stay on the road and rejoin at Instruction 3 '...follow the road round a sharp...'.

2 Climb steeply through woodland. At a track T-junction turn **R** signposted *Culbone Church*. Shortly, at the T-junction with Toll Road turn **L** and follow the road around a sharp **right-hand** hairpin bend signposted *Countisbury, Lynmouth*.

3 At a junction of roads and tracks continue **SA** uphill on a lane signposted *Ash Farm* (i.e. NOT Yarner Farm to the right nor Countisbury to the left). Follow tarmac for almost 2km to its end shortly after sweeping right-hand bend above Silcombe Farm. The good stone track turns to mainly grass over stone base.

4 After 2.2km at the junction with road beyond a gate go **SA** signposted *Bridleway to County Gate and Lynmouth* then shortly **R** (same sign). Follow the narrower, sunken grassy track between walls and through several gates.

5 After 800m go through a gate into an open field by a 4-way wooden post and turn **L** steeply uphill along left-hand field edge signposted *Bridleway to Oareford, County Gate*. Go through a bridlegate and turn **R** parallel with the wall to the right. Stay on the lower faint track close to the wall on the right for 1.3km. Emerge at the road by a white house, cross **SA** onto a track opposite signposted *Bridleway*.

6 Cross the main road (A39) near to the visitor centre and café and turn **L** before the car park through a field gate marked *Bridleway* onto a grassy track. Follow close to the fence on the left to join a more defined path, descending steeply. At the point where the gradient flattens at the bottom of the hill bear **L*** through a bridlegate signposted *Oare Church*. Go through several gates. At the road bear **R**. Cross the bridge, climb and at the T-junction turn **L** signposted *Oareford, Robber's Bridge*.

OR * Or for refreshments continue **SA** to cross footbridge, follow the track to the road then turn **R** to The Buttery Tearoom in Malmsmead.

7 After 3km, **immediately** after crossing narrow stone Robber's Bridge over the river (SS 820464) turn **L** uphill through a gate signposted *Bridleway to Culbone Inn* then turn immediately **R** to continue climbing on an obvious track. Well-graded climb.

8 At the top go through Culbone Inn car park. At the T-junction with the A39 turn **R** then **L** onto the lane signposted *Minehead, Bike Route 51, Yarner Farm*.

9 **Easy to miss:** on a descent, shortly after passing a wide track to the left signposted *Lillycombe Estate* and a track to the right with a *Private, No Right of Way* sign, turn next **R** downhill through a gate signposted *Bridleway to Pittcombe Head*.

10 Follow blue waymarks. Cross the bridge to the other side of the valley and bear **L** to continue downhill on a forest track. **Easy to miss:** just before the trail starts to climb at a track junction by a 3-way wooden post turn **L** through a metal gate signposted *Bridleway to Porlock Weir*. Join tarmac by house and bear **L**.

11 Briefly rejoin the outward route on the hairpin bend. Bear **R** downhill then **easy to miss:** after 250m (keep your brakes on!) bear **R** through a gate by a *Public Path to Porlock Weir* signpost*. Short climb. Follow the red-tipped waymarks and signs for Porlock Ford. At a T-junction of tracks turn **L**. At the T-junction with the road turn **L** to return to Porlock Weir.

OR * There are two other, more technical descents possible, dropping down to the Porlock Weir road: the first starts on the **L** as soon as you leave tarmac and runs parallel with the toll road (a reverse of the outward route), the second **L** comes after a further 700m, signposted to Porlock Weir and starts with brilliant singletrack, contours on a wider rocky track, and then drops sharp left (blue arrow on tree) on more technical singletrack to the road.

⚙ Making a day of it
At the western end of this route, the Brendon & the Doone Valley ride (page 79) is just a stone's throw away in Malmsmead (SS 792477). Alternatively, follow the B3225 east to Porlock for the Porlock & Selworthy Beacon ride (page 91).

14 Porlock to Minehead via Selworthy Beacon

25km

Introduction

The whole of this great lump of land, from Bossington Hill in the west up over Selworthy Beacon to Minehead in the east is like Quantocks-by-the-Sea: broad, stone tracks with excellent drainage through a landscape of heather and fern but with amazing sea views as an added bonus. The woodland descent to Minehead on zigzag tracks is inevitably confusing. The climb back up through lovely Wood Combe gives you the opportunity of reliving it all again, this time heading west.

The Ride

Tracks on the ground, tracks on the map, how infrequently they coincide in areas like this, criss-crossed with a thousand paths. As the ride is largely a ridge ride it shouldn't be too hard to stay in vaguely the right location: drop too far north and you are in the briny and too far south and you'll be run over by a juggernaut on the A39. This is one of the few occasions when the Southwest Coast Path runs along a good quality bridleway so enjoy the views and say hello to the ramblers. The descent into Minehead is confusing and you may well take a different course each time you do it as there are lots of 'balcony' paths linked by zigzag connecting sections. You should be spat out near a roundabout at the end of the road by a café, not far from the Olde Ship Aground pub. The route skirts the edge of Minehead, soon climbing through Higher Town and back along the delightful track through Wood Combe back up to the ridge. This offers more great sea views with a final bonus of gliding down through woodland back to Porlock on the track you may well have walked up to get to the top of Bossington Hill.

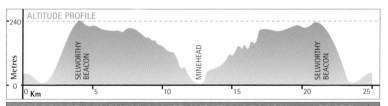

ALTITUDE PROFILE

240

Metres

SELWORTHY BEACON

MINEHEAD

SELWORTHY BEACON

0

0 Km   5   10   15   20   25

PORLOCK TO MINEHEAD VIA SELWORTHY BEACON   GRADE: ▲

TOTAL DISTANCE: 25KM » **TOTAL ASCENT**: 570M » **TIME**: 3–4 HOURS » **START/FINISH**: EAST SIDE OF PORLOCK (BOSSINGTON ROAD) OR MINEHEAD (HARBOUR) » **START GRID REF**: SS 891469 (PORLOCK); SS 970472 (MINEHEAD) **SATNAV**: PORLOCK » **PARKING**: BOSSINGTON ROAD, PORLOCK (ON THE WIDE SECTIONS NEAR TO THE A39) OR MINEHEAD HARBOUR » **OS MAP**: EXPLORER OL9 » **PUB**: LOTS OF CHOICE IN PORLOCK AND MINEHEAD » **CAFÉ**: LOTS OF CHOICE IN PORLOCK AND MINEHEAD

14 PORLOCK TO MINEHEAD VIA SELWORTHY BEACON

Directions – Porlock to Minehead via Selworthy Beacon

6 Follow Bossington Road northeast away from Porlock and the A39. **Ignore** a lane to the left by a Holnicote Estate sign. Go past the church.

2 At a large triangle of grass turn **R** signposted *Allerford*. After 450m take the second **L**, just after a second church signposted *Bridleway to Selworthy Beacon*.

3 Go past thatched houses, bear **L** and keep following blue waymarks and signs for *Selworthy Beacon*. Steep woodland climb. At a T-junction of tracks by a 3-way signpost and a small wooden bench turn **L** signposted *Bridleway to Selworthy Beacon*. The gradient eases.

4 At next T-junction, with a *Lynch* sign pointing back where you have come from, turn **R** to continue uphill. Turn **R** again at the T-junction with a *Coast Path* sign (acorn symbol). **Remember these two junctions for the return route.**

5 After 500m turn **L** on the lower path signposted *Coast Path*. Huge views west to dramatic cliffs, north to Wales, east to the island of Flat Holm. Keep following *Coast Path* signs. At crossroads with the lane (SS 926484) go **SA** signposted *Minehead* (acorn symbol).

6 Follow the main track on a variety of surfaces for 2.5km. After a climb then a descent, at a 5-way post by a wooden bench (near to the car parking area to the right), bear **L** signposted *Minehead Seafront*.

7 Superb descending track with great views. Go past a square concrete parking area then past a low concrete building to the left. Follow the main wide track. This briefly turns to tarmac. Immediately after wooden stakes in path, at a multi-junction of paths by a 4-way post, with a red-tiled house about 100m ahead, turn sharp **L** downhill signposted *Bridleway to Culver Cliff*.

8 Join a better stone (vehicle) track and turn sharp **R** then almost immediately sharp **L** just after a wooden barrier, to continue steeply downhill on the lower track. At the next similar junction turn sharp **R** on a downhill zigzag track by a wooden bench.

9 Emerge at the turning circle on the seafront. Follow the seafront for 800m past the Old Ship Aground pub, cafés, harbour and the 'Hands' sculpture holding a map marking the start of the South West Coast Path. Take the first road on the **R** after the Quay Inn signposted *Town Centre, Hospital, Blenheim Gardens* onto Blenheim Road. Shortly, at a 5-way junction of roads bear **R** onto a narrow street (Quay Lane) running to the left of a tall, red stone wall.

10 Go up the steps at the end of lane and turn **R** uphill on a broad road to go round a sharp left-hand hairpin bend by the memorial cross. Go past the church. Maintain or gain height, ignoring turnings. Follow the road around a long sweeping left-hand bend then a sharper right-hand bend. Immediately after the cattle grid, before the gradient steepens further, turn **L** on a broad stone track signposted *Bridleway to North Hill*.

11 Shortly, **ignore** a tarmac path to the left then at a fork bear **R** on the upper track. At a junction of tracks by a small (water company) building bear **L** to pass close to the compound fence on a contouring track. Superb views down into the wooded combe to the left.

12 At a T-junction of tracks bear **L** downhill then shortly turn **R** for a very steep push on grass to the road. Turn **R** for 100m then **L** through the car parking area to rejoin the outward route at a 5-way signpost. Turn **L** and follow *Coast Path* signs, passing through several bridlegates.

13 Follow the Coast Path for 4km. Leave this at a *Lynch Combe* signpost (SS 911483). Turn **L** here then shortly **L** again signposted *Lynch*. There is shortly a third **L** turn back into the valley to your left (i.e. do not plummet down towards the sea).

14 After contouring turn **R** downhill by the wooden bench. Steep, testing descent. At the T-junction with the road turn **R** and follow signs back to Porlock.

◄◎◯ Making a day of it
Horner Wood (page 97) lies just to the south of Porlock. The Porlock Weir & County Gate ride (page 85) starts just 4km west of Porlock.

15 Horner Wood

10km

Introduction

Everything about this ride is extreme. It is extremely short, the climbs are extremely tough, the descents are extremely steep and the whole woodland is extremely beautiful. It is also one of those rides where there are masses of tracks on the ground not shown on the map, so those with local knowledge will probably wonder why it has missed out so many delights. The sad answer – this is 100% legal, only using bridleways and permitted paths.

The Ride

There ain't much flat in this ride so enjoy the relatively gentle contouring track taking you from Horner around the edge of the woodland to the base of Crawter Hill (or should that be Crawl-up Hill?). What would normally be an easily-missed turning shouldn't present a problem as you crawl past it at about 5kph. Flora's Ride beckons, one of several named walks or rides in the woods, including Granny's Ride, Lord Ebrington's Ride and Stags Path. The descent to cross Horner Water should get the brakes squealing and as for the climb... Hey, sniff the breeze and listen to the birdsong, this is meant to be fun! A reasonably flat section above the tree line takes you through several fields with fine views over the dense, almost tropical woodland before a second testing zigzag descent to cross East Water Valley. Sense finally prevails and you can follow the valley floor track back to the start. All over so soon? Try a second lap.

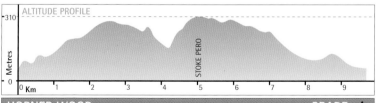

HORNER WOOD   GRADE: ▲

TOTAL DISTANCE: 10KM » **TOTAL ASCENT**: 430M » **TIME**: 1.5–2 HOURS » **START/FINISH**: HORNER, SOUTHEAST OF PORLOCK » **START GRID REF**: SS 898455 » **SATNAV**: TA24 8HY » **PARKING**: HORNER CAR PARK, OFF THE A39 SOUTHEAST OF PORLOCK » **OS MAP**: EXPLORER OL9 » **PUB**: NONE ON ROUTE, NEAREST IN PORLOCK **CAFÉ**: HORNER VALE TEAROOM, HORNER, TEL: 01643 862 506

MAKING A SPLASH THROUGH EAST WATER

15 HORNER WOOD

Directions – Horner Wood

↪ Exit the Horner car park, turn **L** then **R** onto a track signposted *Bridleway to Porlock* to cross the bridge. **Ignore** the footpath to the left. Follow the perimeter fence above the campsite. At a fork of tracks about 100m after the end of the campsite bear **L** uphill away from the field and fence to your right.

2 At the road turn **L** then shortly **L** again on a lane, steeply uphill.

3 Ignore a bridleway to the right to Porlock then shortly, on a right-hand bend, bear **L** onto a stone and earth track to the **L** signposted *Flora's Ride, Bridleway to Stoke Pero*. Shortly, follow the loose stone/red earth track to the **R**, ignoring a tempting contouring grass track ahead.

4 Climb to the summit. **Easy to miss:** after 100m, as the track swings right, turn sharp **L** downhill and enter the oak woodland. Descend to a T-junction at a 3-way wooden post and turn **R** signposted *Granny's Ride* (blue waymark). Fine singletrack.

5 At a diagonal crossroads of tracks go **SA** downhill on Granny's Ride, crossing Lord Ebrington's Path. Great descent to cross the bridge over the river. Keep following signs for Granny's Ride and Stoke Pero.

6 Very steep push up from the bridge. At T-junction at the top of the steepest section of the climb bear **R** to continue climbing more gently signposted *Bridleway to Stoke Pero*.

7 Exit the woodland via a wooden gate and turn sharp **L** towards a gap in the stone wall signposted *Bridleway to Webber's Post*. At the next gateway (in a dip) continue in the same direction with the hedge now to your right, soon joining a more well-defined grassy track with blue waymarks. Stay close to the fence/hedgerow to your right.

8 Go through a metal gate then shortly through a wooden gate next to a stile. Follow the right-hand field edge with the wall and fence to your right. **Ignore** a sharp left (signposted *Permitted footpath to Stoke Pero*). Follow the bridleway **SA** then shortly bear **L** at a grassy fork between two old silver birches on the lower track.

9 More fine singletrack zigzagging downhill. Cross the stream and bear **L** onto a rocky track in the valley bottom, ignoring a signed bridleway leading off right steeply uphill. Follow the rocky track down the valley, bearing around **L** to cross East Water then Horner Water – either by increasingly wet water splashes, or by carrying briefly over footbridges. Shortly after crossing Horner Water turn **R** onto a more defined track that runs parallel to Horner Water down the valley (north) back to the start. (Please be aware that there will be more walkers on this stretch and ride with due consideration.) After a final gate, turn **R** over the bridge, **L** at the road, and **R** – shortly thereafter – back into the car park.

◄●OO Making a day of it

Horner is close enough to Porlock to link easily to the Porlock & Selworthy Beacon ride (page 91) or to the Porlock Weir & County Gate ride (page 85). About 5km of quiet, steep lanes southwest from Stoke Pero will take you to the Winsford & Exford ride (page 109) at SS 856404.

16 Withypool & the Sportsman's Inn   22km

Introduction

Quite possibly the finest ride in the heart of the moorland with a sprinkling of everything – tearoom and pub at the start/finish, excellent views, good quality tracks, a pub in the very middle of nowhere and enough rough stuff to make you feel you've had an outing. And could you resist a ride that takes you past a place called Tudball's Splats?!

The Ride

Withypool is a picture postcard, thatched village in the heart of Exmoor, much loved by second homeowners. A civilised climb along a dead end road takes you to the start of one of the most beautiful tracks on all of Exmoor, dropping down into the Barle Valley where a conveniently placed footbridge saves you being swept downstream to Exeter. There are great tree roots on this ride - Tolkien would have loved them. The section between Horsen Farm and Sherdon Farm is one of fields, gates and blue waymarks, before rejoining a broad stone-based track that descends then climbs to the road and the extraordinarily located Sportsman's Inn. Back off-road, everything is just too easy as you zoom down to cross Willingford Bridge and climb the other side on good tracks. Exmoor bites back. There is a rough moorland section beyond the unusual Porchester Post monument. Still, you are on your way downhill now and the going just gets better as you descend back to cream tea heaven.

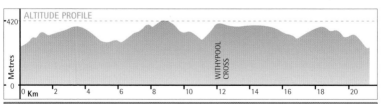

ALTITUDE PROFILE

Metres | 420 | 0

0 Km — 2 — 4 — 6 — 8 — 10 — 12 — 14 — 16 — 18 — 20

WITHYPOOL CROSS

WITHYPOOL & THE SPORTSMAN'S INN   GRADE: ▲

TOTAL DISTANCE: 22KM » **TOTAL ASCENT**: 460M » **TIME**: 2.5–3.5 HOURS » **START/FINISH**: WITHYPOOL
START GRID REF: SS 845354 » **SATNAV**: TA24 7QP » **PARKING**: CAR PARK IN THE CENTRE OF WITHYPOOL
OS MAP: EXPLORER OL9 » **PUB**: SPORTSMAN'S INN, TEL: 01643 831 109 » **CAFÉ**: BRING SANDWICHES

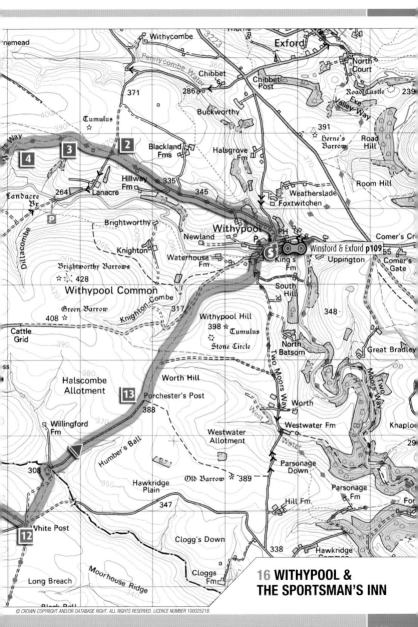

16 WITHYPOOL & THE SPORTSMAN'S INN

Directions – Withypool & the Sportsman's Inn

⌕➤ Exit the Withypool car park and turn **L**. Cross the bridge, go through the village and turn **L** immediately before the Royal Oak pub. After 150m take the first **L** onto a no through road signposted *Westerclose House*. Steady climb on tarmac which turns to track at the gate.

2 At crossroads with a lane go **SA** onto a continuation of the track signposted *Bridleway to Simonside*.

3 There are many tracks on the ground not marked on the map. You are following signs for *Two Moors Way* (shown as 'MW'). **Ignore** tracks to the left leading towards gates into the adjoining field. After 800m at a fork of tracks by a 3-way signpost bear **L** signposted *Simonsbath via Cow Castle*.

4 Superb grassy descent with magnificent views. Go down through several gates into woodland to join a fine broad stone track. May be muddy through a small coniferous plantation (look for better alternatives to right and left).

5 At the ford continue on the same side of the river for 50m to cross via a bridge, signposted *Blue Gate*. Cross a second, small footbridge and turn **R** uphill on the main stone track away from the river. Climb alongside a line of trees then enter an enclosed canopy of trees.

6 Cross a small ford and continue climbing. At the road turn **L** then almost immediately **L** again through double gates onto a wide gravel track. At the next gate climb diagonally **L** across the field to another gate (indistinct track) towards the left of the line of trees on the horizon.

7 Go through a gate in the stone and earth wall and diagonally **L** again uphill (**do not** turn right immediately after the gate alongside the fence on the right – this is rough, wet and boggy) towards a field gate in the wire fence. Go over the brow of the hill and descend on an obvious earth and stone track towards the gate in the line of trees / hedgerow.

8 Follow the field edge and blue waymarks through two fields then at a T-junction with a broad, enclosed track turn **L** signposted *Bridleway to Sherdon* (this is on a low signpost ahead and to your left).

9 Go past the remote house at Sherdon. Descend to cross the river then climb.

10 At the T-junction with the road turn **R** then shortly, at Withypool Cross, bear **R** again signposted *North & South Molton*.

11 Go past the Sportsman's Inn then after 200m take the first road **L** signposted *Twitchen, Molland*. After 800m, at the crossroads of lanes (your priority) at Mudgate Cross, turn first **L** signposted *National Cycle Network Route 3*.

12 Fast descent. At the junction beyond a cattlegrid turn sharp **L** gently uphill on a broad stone track. Descend to cross bridge then go **SA** uphill signposted *Byway to Withypool*.

13 Go past Porchester Post. At the T-junction with the road bear **R** uphill onto a track signposted *Byway to Withypool*. At the road turn **L** downhill to return to the start.

◄▭ Making a day of it
A steep climb east of Withypool to Comer's Cross (SS 860355) links to the Winsford & Exford ride (page 109). If you want to experience one of the best lane ridge rides in the whole of the UK, from Sandyway Cross (SS 793332) near to the Sportsman's Inn, follow the road northwest to Mole's Chamber (SS 717394). This is best done on a day of excellent visibility.

17 Winsford & Exford

Introduction

Linked by the infant River Exe, Winsford and Exford are two of the main villages in the centre of Exmoor and both boast stores, pubs and tearooms. This ride has a bit of everything from rough moorland to rollercoaster stone bedrock descent, fearsome climbs and gentle riverside tracks.

The Ride

With one exception all the roads and tracks out of Winsford turn into a steep climb sooner or later. In this case it is sooner. You're barely past the thatched Royal Oak pub and the gradient goes vertical, the start of a 200m climb up onto Winsford Hill. Off-road, the ride runs close to the rim of the dramatically concave Punchbowl. As there are many tracks on the ground you may or

may not emerge at the road at the right place to continue towards Knaplock but search and you will find the track before long. Beyond the farm this is raw Exmoor, with a bit of boggy ground thrown in for good measure. Regain the road briefly before setting off across moorland again to discover a fine descent down to Exford. A steep climb beyond the bustle of Exford takes you back up above 400m and the start of a descent that gets better and better, ending with a smooth stone rollercoaster and gates that mysteriously open at the press of a button... A mixture of tarmac, concrete, grass, stone and earth, finishing with a long, easy riverside stretch brings you back to the delights of Winsford.

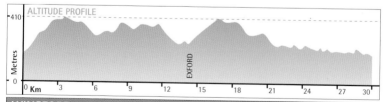

ALTITUDE PROFILE

410

Metres

0

0 Km   3   6   9   12   15   18   21   24   27   30

EXFORD

WINSFORD & EXFORD   GRADE: ▲

TOTAL DISTANCE: 30KM » **TOTAL ASCENT**: 460M » **TIME**: 3–4 HOURS » **START/FINISH**: WINSFORD » **START GRID REF**: SS 906349 » **SATNAV**: TA24 7JE » **PARKING**: IN THE CENTRE OF WINSFORD » **OS MAP**: EXPLORER OL9 **PUB**: ROYAL OAK, WINSFORD, TEL: 01643 851 455; EXMOOR WHITE HORSE, EXFORD, TEL: 01643 831 229; CROWN HOTEL, EXFORD, TEL: 01643 831 554 » **CAFÉ**: LOTS OF CHOICE IN EXFORD

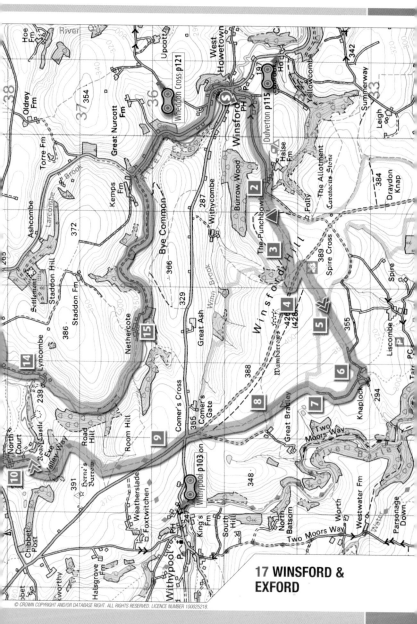

17 WINSFORD & EXFORD

Directions – Winsford & Exford

⊙► From the centre of Winsford go past the Royal Oak pub.

2 Climb steeply then steadily for 1.5km. Shortly after the cattle grid, on a left-hand bend, bear **R** uphill away from the road on a broad stone track that soon turns to grass signposted *Bridleway to Winsford Hill & Tarr Steps*.

3 Many tracks, few shown on the map. Continue climbing, bearing **L** at the first fork away from the woodland on the right and soon following the edge of a deep gully (the Punchbowl) down to your right. Maintain or gain height at each junction then towards the end of the Punchbowl fork **L** at two junctions. (If you find yourself *descending* alongside the rim of the Punchbowl you have gone too far.)

4 You should emerge at the road at a *Winsford via Punchbowl* signpost* pointing back where you have come from. (*If you arrive at tarmac and the road is climbing the hill to the left, turn **L** uphill until arriving at the signs mentioned above.) Turn **L** on tarmac for 300m then, **easy to miss:** opposite a 3-way wooden post turn **R** signposted *Bridleway to Knaplock* onto an earth and stone track, descending through gorse.

5 After 150m at a fork of grassy tracks bear **R** on the upper track, maintaining height and aiming towards the right-hand end of the line of trees ahead. Join the trees at a wall/hedgerow corner and a second *Bridleway to Knaplock* signpost. Continue in the same direction with the trees to the right. Exit the corner of the field via a gate (blue waymark).

6 Continue in the same direction as the field edge becomes a stone track. At the T-junction with a concrete track turn **R**. At the T-junction with the corrugated roof barn of Higher Knaplock Farm ahead turn **R** signposted *Bridleway to Tarr Steps*. At the second farm (Knaplock) turn **R** again signposted *Withypool via Comers Gate*.

7 Follow the enclosed track and blue paint waymarks. With a *No Public Right of Way* sign on a field gate ahead, turn **R** following the stream bed/stone-based track which turns to a grassy track. Follow signs for *Bridleway avoiding bog* on a rough track.

8 Bear **R** onto a better track near to a farm. **Ignore** a left turn to the River Barle. At the T-junction with the B3223 by a cattlegrid turn **L**.

9 Climb to the brow. **Easy to miss:** about 100m after passing a large gravel parking area on the left keep an eye out for a gate in the hedgerow to the **R** signposted *Bridleway to Exford*. Follow the **left-hand** field edge through several gates then at 3-way wooden post after a steep grassy descent turn **L** signposted *Bridleway* through gates and across a level field. Good, testing stone descent with drop-offs then a muddy track.

10 Join tarmac and continue in the same direction between houses signposted *Bridleway to County Road*. At the T-junction with the road bear **R** downhill. At the bottom of the hill turn **R** onto the B3224 into Exford, cross the bridge over the River Exe, turn **L** by the Crown Hotel and Exmoor Stores signposted *Cloutsham, Porlock* then first **R** onto Coombe Lane (no through road).

11 Climb steeply, ignoring right turns. Tarmac turns to track and continues to climb. Keep following *Bridleway* signs and blue waymarks, eventually crossing a field between fences. At a T-junction with a wide stone track turn **R** downhill signposted *Prescott Down*.

12 Follow the main stone-based track across moorland. Go past a large granite memorial stone and through a gate onto an enclosed track. Fine rollercoaster bedrock stream bed. Push button gates to exit onto the road!

13 At the crossroads with the B3224 go **SA** signposted *Winsford, Dulverton*. After 550m take the first road to the **R** (no sign). **Ignore** a farm entrance to the right. Take the next **R** onto a stone track by a *Bridleway to Lyncombe* signpost.

14 At the bottom of a steep concrete section turn **L** by a house on your left. This soon turns to track. Follow in the same direction over a variety of surfaces from good broad stone track to rougher field sections with occasional muddy sections.

15 Go through several gates close to Nethercote then along an easy riverside stretch on a broad stone and gravel track. At the T-junction with the road turn **R** and follow for 2km back to the start in Winsford.

⛓ Making a day of it

Two other rides start from or pass through Winsford: you could go south on the Dulverton to Winsford ride (page 115) or north on the Winsford to Wheddon Cross ride (page 121).

18 Dulverton to Winsford

Introduction

With the exception of the towns on the north coast (Lynton, Lynmouth and Porlock) Dulverton is the largest settlement on Exmoor, with several pubs, shops and cafés and the Exmoor National Park HQ. The ride has a bit of everything – good stone tracks, easy climbs, impossible climbs, hair-raising descents, breezalong descents plus a bit of tricky route finding. And a good pub and tearoom in Winsford.

The Ride

The stone-based 180m climb from Dulverton north to Higher Broford is largely rideable with ever better views opening up into the Exe Valley to the east and towards the heart of the moor to the west. Finding the route past Highercombe Farm to the B3223 can be a bit tricky but if you keep heading west you'll get there. You may find similar problems locating the start of the bridleway that drops down to Winsford but it is worth finding! Testing singletrack through woodland leads on to a stone rollercoaster after Yellowcombe Cottage into the pretty village of Winsford. The climb up Edbrooke Hill is so steep that you might as well eat and drink well in Winsford - you won't be able to ride up it. More tricky route-finding brings you to some atmospheric ruins down in the valley near the thud thud thud of a water pump. Climb back to join the outward route but take a different, long, wonderful enclosed stone descent back to Dulverton.

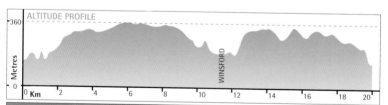

ALTITUDE PROFILE

360

Metres

WINSFORD

0

Km   2   4   6   8   10   12   14   16   18   20

DULVERTON TO WINSFORD

GRADE: ▲

TOTAL DISTANCE: 20KM » **TOTAL ASCENT**: 470M » **TIME**: 2.5–3.5 HOURS » **START/FINISH**: DULVERTON
START GRID REF: SS 912279 » **SATNAV**: TA22 9EX » **PARKING**: MAIN PAY & DISPLAY CAR PARK IN DULVERTON
OS MAP: EXPLORER OL9 » **PUB**: LOTS OF CHOICE IN DULVERTON; ROYAL OAK, WINSFORD, TEL: 01643 851 362
CAFÉ: LOTS OF CHOICE IN DULVERTON; KARSLAKE HOUSE, WINSFORD, TEL: 01643 851 242

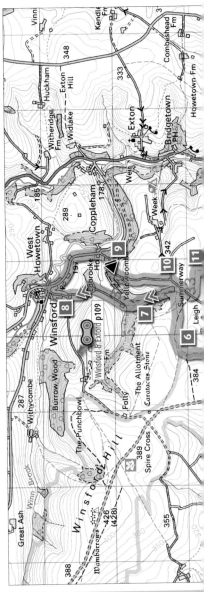

18 DULVERTON TO WINSFORD

↪ From the Lion Hotel in the centre of Dulverton take the B3223 towards Lynton and Exford. **Easy to miss:** after 1.6km bear **R** onto a no through road by a house sign for Sweetoaks signposted *RUPP to Court Down*. Shortly fork **R** (i.e. do NOT go over the cattlegrid). Climb on a stone-based vehicle track with a canopy of trees overhead.

2 At a T-junction of tracks at the top of the climb turn **L** signposted *Winsford*. Go through a gate onto a broad stone track and shortly fork **R** onto the upper track by a severely pruned oak tree.

3 Shortly after the summit, at a crossroads of tracks turn **L** onto tarmac signposted *Winsford*. **Easy to miss:** after 800m keep an eye out for a blue paint waymark on a bridlegate off to the **L**, set back from the road, adjacent to a metal field gate (SS 908316). Go through the gate onto a climbing grassy track with ever better views.

4 Go through a bridlegate after passing Highercombe Farm buildings to your left and follow signs for *Tarr Steps* diagonally **R** on a grassy track.

5 Follow the track to the road, turn **R**, cross the cattlegrid then opposite the second road on the left (to Tarr Steps) turn **R** downhill onto a grassy track, with a line of trees to your **R**. There is the occasional blue paint waymark on trees.

6 Follow to the wall corner and continue downhill towards woodland on a better red gravel track. Follow with a line of trees to the left. At a metal gate go into the field to the **L** via a bridlegate, leaving the main stone track. Follow the **left-hand** field edge around two sides of the field, **ignoring** two bridlegates in the corner of the field. Take the **next** gate on the **L**, opposite a *Week Lane/Tarr Steps* signpost.

7 Descend on a steep, at times narrow, track signposted *Bridleway* through a pheasant-rearing area and down through woodland, deciduous then conifer. Ford the stream near the footbridge and turn **R** through a gate to join a wider track. Climb then descend on a bedrock rollercoaster track.

8 At the T-junction with the road turn **R** down into Winsford. At the T-junction just past the Royal Oak pub turn **R** then shortly **R** again in the centre of the village signposted *Dulverton, Minehead*.

9 After 1km, at the bottom of a dip on a left-hand bend, shortly after a *Bends Ahead* sign, turn **R** onto a broad stone track signposted *Byway to Edbrooke Hill Gate*. Ignore the first track to the right. Very steep climb. At the crossroads of tracks turn **R** signposted *Week Lane*.

10 At the T-junction with the road turn **R**. Climb. **Easy to miss:** 150m after the summit turn **L** through a gravel parking area and a metal gate (blue waymark) onto a wide grassy track (SS 905329) signposted *Bridleway to Broford*.

11 At the end of the field turn **R** through a gate signposted *Bridleway*. Follow enclosed track, always staying on the lower option, dropping down to cross the stream near to the pumping engine. At the top of a short climb leave the main track and turn **R** uphill through the right-hand of two gates into field by a *Bridleway* signpost.

12 Climb alongside the fence (to your left) towards a clump of trees on the horizon. Go through a gate onto a broad stone track. Descend on a broad smooth track. At the junction of several tracks by farm buildings turn **R** onto a level track signposted *Byway to Higher Broford*. Descend, climb, then, at a T-junction with a similar broad track, turn sharp **R** to continue uphill signposted *Byway*.

13 At the crossroads with tarmac ahead turn **L** gently uphill on a broad stone track signposted *Byway to Dulverton* to rejoin the outward route. Continue on the main track for 3.6km, **ignoring** the track to the right you climbed up from Dulverton. Great descent, some muddy patches. Emerge at School Lane by Rock House Inn, and turn **R** to return to the start.

⊶☉☉ **Making a day of it**

In Winsford you can link to the Winsford & Exford ride (page 109) and the Winsford to Wheddon Cross ride (page 119). Less than 3km on lanes heading east from Dulverton brings you to the Wimbleball Reservoir ride (page 129) at SS 945275.

19 Winsford to Wheddon Cross

27km

Introduction

Set right in the heart of Exmoor this ride is nevertheless one of fields, farms and woodland rather than rough, exposed moorland. There are several very fine descents, some stony and technical, others grassy and open.

The Ride

A series of climbs and descents, on lanes and stone tracks, take you north from Winsford, with one memorable stone rollercoaster down into Luckwell Bridge. Climb to Wheddon Cross, Exmoor's highest village, on a narrow track, with the chance of a beer in the pub or snacks from the stores. More lanes take you to the top of one of the best technical descents in Exmoor down

Putham Lane to the ford – definitely one to come back to. You are faced with a climb of almost 250m from Putham Ford up to the highpoint of the ride on Lype Hill and the radio masts, setting you up nicely for the long descent down to Brompton Regis, with one very fine open grass downhill before a short, grim mudbath near King's Brompton Farm. Climb steeply from Brompton Regis to Combeshead Cross for one of those timeless track descents through fields and woodland to Badgers Holt pub on the A396. If it has been particularly wet it is worth using the A396 for about 1km to avoid a potentially very muddy track on the other side of the Exe to get you back to the start.

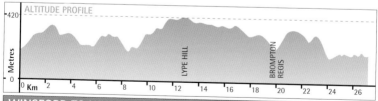

WINSFORD TO WHEDDON CROSS   GRADE: ▲

TOTAL DISTANCE: 27KM » **TOTAL ASCENT**: 570M » **TIME**: 3–4 HOURS » **START/FINISH**: WINSFORD
START GRID REF: SS 906349 » **SATNAV**: TA24 7JE » **PARKING**: IN THE CENTRE OF WINSFORD » **OS MAP**: EXPLORER OL9
PUB: REST & BE THANKFUL, WHEDDON CROSS, TEL: 01643 841 222; BADGERS HOLT, BRIDGETOWN, TEL: 01643 851 204
CAFÉ: PULHAM'S MILL TEAROOM, BROMPTON REGIS, TEL: 01398 371366

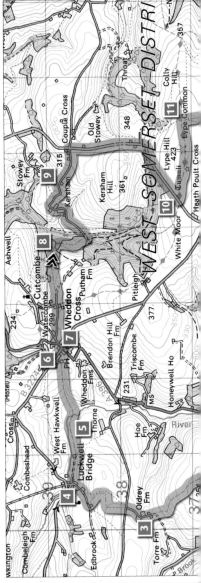

19 WINSFORD TO WHEDDON CROSS

➲ From the car park in the centre of Winsford follow signs for *Exford* and *Simonsbath*. After 350m, towards the end of the village, take the first road uphill to the **R** opposite a white house with a tall wall.

2 Steep climb. After 800m **ignore** a 3-way track to the left by a barn. After 350m, at the summit, take the next **L** by a tall, metal barn onto a broad stone track signposted *Bridleway to Luckwell Bridge via Oldrey Lane*. Climb then descend.

3 At the road bear **R**. At the crossroads with a lane go **SA** onto a sunken stone track signposted *Byway to Luckwell Bridge*. Excellent stone rollercoaster descent.

4 At the T-junction with road at the bottom turn **R** gently downhill. At the bottom of the hill just before a humpback bridge turn **R** onto a stone track signposted *Bridleway to Wheddon Cross*.

5 At the fork of tracks with a house ahead take the upper **right-hand** track (same sign). Stay parallel to the stream on the left. Cross the river via ford or bridge then after 30m bear **R** through field gate (blue waymark) onto a sunken track, climbing between hedgerows.

6 At the top of the enclosed track go **SA** through gravel car park and along the **left-hand** edge of the playing field ahead and through the main Wheddon Cross car park.

7 At the crossroads in the centre of Wheddon Cross by the pub turn **L** on the A396 towards Dunster then first **R** by the war memorial signposted *Cutcombe only*. Shortly turn **R** again signposted *Putham* then after 450m, on a sharp left-hand bend, bear **R** onto a no through road signposted *Byway to Luxborough via Putham Ford*.

8 Just before the cattlegrid bear **L** onto a wide, stone track signposted *Putham Lane*. At a crossroads of tracks go **SA** downhill on a continuation of the sunken track. Fantastic rollercoaster stone track descent. Cross the stream and climb steeply, following *Kersham Lane, Couple Cross* signs.

9 The gradient eases. Descend past an isolated farm then long climb on track/narrow tarmac lane. At the offset crossroads at the Couple Cross signpost turn **R** gently uphill.

10 **Easy to miss:** after almost 2km, and just after the brow of the hill, turn **L** through a metal field gate (blue waymark on left-hand gatepost) by a small gravel area at the side of the road (SS 943372). Go diagonally **L** across the field towards the gate on the horizon.

11 Continue through several gates with blue waymarks, passing to the **L** of the trig point, alongside a fence on your right, then aim diagonally **R** across the field towards the mast. Pass to the **L** of the cluster of buildings then bear **R** downhill to go through a gate in the hedgerow. Join a forest road and continue **SA** signposted *Bridleway to Kennisham Hill*.

12 At the crossroads with the B3224 go **SA** onto the road opposite, signposted *Brompton Regis, Dulverton*. After passing Goosemoor Cottage on your right, **ignore** a footpath to Gupworthy and take the next broad stone track to the **L** signposted *Bridleway to Brompton Regis*.

13 After 1.3km as the main track swings left, bear **R** (in effect **SA**) through a metal gate onto a wide grassy track, then shortly through another gate (blue waymark). Bear slightly **L** downhill to a gate in the earth and stone wall/hedgerow. Short, overgrown, muddy section by gate and woodland near King's Brompton Farm. Continue in the same direction along the **right-hand** field edge to emerge at the road and bear **R**.

14 **Easy to miss:** on a sharp left-hand bend at the bottom of a fast tarmac descent (SS 957314) turn **R** onto a track signposted *Byway to Brompton Regis*. Just before the barns turn **L** downhill, cross the stream via the bridge or ford. At the T-junction with the road turn **R**. After the church in Brompton Regis turn **R** signposted *Unsuitable for motors*.

15 Steep climb. At Combeshead Cross turn **R** then shortly take the first **L** on concrete track signposted *Bridleway to Bridgetown, Combeshead Farm*.

16 Go through the farmyard and a gate set between walls. Descend along the **right-hand** field edge aiming for a bridlegate tucked into the **right-hand** corner. Short overgrown section to cross a wooden bridge and climb to a second bridlegate. Turn **L** between some barns on the right and the farm on the left. Climb on a good stone track.

17 At a crossroads of bridleways by a 5-way signpost go **SA** through a metal gate opposite then bear **L** along the left-hand field edge. At the end of the field take the **left-hand** of two gates (blue waymark). After 100m bear **R** through a bridlegate steeply downhill, diagonally across the field to a field gate with a blue waymark. Continue in the same direction past an oak tree to another blue waymarked gate into the woodland.

18 At the T-junction with a major forest track bear **L** (blue waymark). At crossroads with a smooth forest road go **SA** signposted *Bridleway to Bridgetown*. Continue downhill more steeply past a house on the left onto a narrow stone track (may be muddy). Emerge at the road at Badgers Holt pub. Turn **R** on the A396 then first **L*** onto Week Lane (a no through road) by Chapel Cottage.

> **OR** * If it has been particularly wet, stay on the A396 for about 1km and take the next road to the left and follow this back to Winsford.

19 Cross the humpback bridge over the river then turn **R** on a broad stone track signposted *Bridleway to Coppleham* (**not** the campsite). At the road turn **L** to return to Winsford.

Making a day of it

Link south to the Dulverton to Winsford ride (page 115) or west to the Winsford & Exford ride (page 109). To the southeast, less than 3km on lanes south from Brompton Regis bring you to the Wimbleball Reservoir ride (page 129) at Hartford (SS 959293).

20 Wimbleball Reservoir

22km

Introduction

The long and testing descent down Haddon Lane about halfway round is the star of the piece, with the rest of the ride a beautiful potter around the largest reservoir on Exmoor with little to trouble even novices.

The Ride

Leave behind the daytrippers as you climb past South Greenslade Farm, descend to cross the reservoir dam then climb up to the top of Haddon Hill. This is the highpoint, at over 300m, which means that you are now faced with a descent. And what a descent! Clearly work has been done to improve the drainage down this wonderful sunken track, which drops 180m down to the River Haddeo at Bury. The next section qualifies as family-friendly: traffic-free and flat alongside the river with a thousand pheasants fattening up for their yearly showdown with the guns. A hidden footbridge saves you getting your feet wet as you join the track that climbs steeply up to the dam (briefly joining the earlier part of the ride) before swooping down to the waterside and climbing through lovely broadleaf woodland to the road. The next section is as close as you can ride legally to the reservoir, although mainly on lanes. Cross the bridge over the northern spur of the lake then follow the permissive trail alongside the water back to the start.

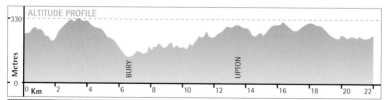

ALTITUDE PROFILE

330

Metres

0

0 Km   2   4   6   8   10   12   14   16   18   20   22

BURY

UPTON

WIMBLEBALL RESERVOIR　　　　　　　　　　　　GRADE: ▲

TOTAL DISTANCE: 22KM » TOTAL ASCENT: 400M » TIME: 2-3 HOURS » START/FINISH: WIMBLEBALL RESERVOIR
START GRID REF: SS 966308 » SATNAV: TA22 9NU » PARKING: WIMBLEBALL RESERVOIR » OS MAP: EXPLORER OL9
PUB: NONE ON ROUTE – NEAREST IN DULVERTON » CAFÉ: BRING SANDWICHES

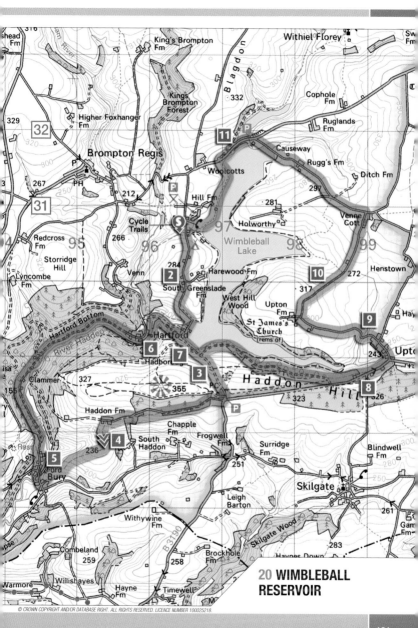

20 WIMBLEBALL RESERVOIR

Directions – Wimbleball Reservoir

➤ From the car park by the main Wimbleball Reservoir visitor centre return to the road, turn **L** onto the no through road signposted *Farm access only*.

2 **Easy to miss:** climb, then shortly after the summit, bear **R** off tarmac uphill onto a broad stone track signposted *Bridleway to Haddon Hill & Hartford*. At a crossroads of tracks turn **L** on a level concrete track (bike route sign) then turn **R** to cross the dam. At the T-junction at the end of the dam turn **L** uphill signposted *Lady Harriet's Drive, Upton*.

3 Long steady climb on tarmac. Cross the cattlegrid, turn **R** at the junction with the road then immediately **R** again onto a wide stone track.

4 After 1.7km, go past farm buildings then bear **L** at a 2-way signpost *Bridleway to Bury* to go through a wooden gate onto a narrow sunken track. Great descent, a few tricky drop-offs. Slippery when wet.

5 At the T-junction with the road in the village of Bury turn **R**. Cross the river via the ford or old stone bridge and bear **R** onto a no through road. This shortly turns to a broad stone track. Follow this easy riverside track for 3.2km, passing a fish farm towards the end.

6 At a junction of tracks after the fish farm bear **R** downhill signposted *Bridleway to Upton*. Follow the obvious track between fences. At the river turn **L**, cross via the footbridge and turn **L** to rejoin the bridleway.

7 Short rough grassy section. Follow signs for *Upton* onto Lady Harriet's Drive, soon bearing **R** uphill on a concrete track. Climb steeply to the dam and continue **SA** on a tarmac track (this short section is used in both loops). About 300m after passing the dam, bear **L** downhill onto a broad stone track by a grit bin and a *Bridleway* signpost. Grassy swoop down to the reservoir then climb through woodland and several gates.

8 At the road bear **L** downhill on a fast descent then shortly take the first road to the **L** signposted *Brompton Regis*. Go down then up. After 350m, on a sharp right-hand bend, bear **L** onto a no through road.

9 Down then up. After 1.3km, just **after** an *Upton Farm, Top Court* sign and just **before** the church, turn **R** uphill onto a stony track signposted *Private Road, Bridlepath only*.

10 Climb then descend. Track turns to tarmac. At the T-junction with the road turn **L**. **Ignore** a left turn to Holworthy.

11 Fast descent. At the T-junction at Besom Cross turn **L** signposted *Brompton Regis, Dulverton*. Cross the bridge over the reservoir then **easy to miss** after 300m turn **L** through a bridlegate next to a field gate signposted *Bike Route*. Follow the main track parallel to the shoreline. At a fork bear **R** to return to the car park at the start.

⊶⊙⊙ Making a day of it

It is about 3km west from Bury to Dulverton to join the Dulverton to Winsford ride (page 115). Alternatively go north from Hartford for 3km to Brompton Regis to join the Winsford to Wheddon Cross ride (page 121).

21 Carhampton & Croydon Hill

17km

Introduction

This is a ride which could be endlessly tweaked as it spends a lot of time in the large Forestry Commission holding on Croydon Hill where there are hundreds of options for singletrack exploration. Carhampton is linked to the forest by some wide stone tracks. The views from the highpoint in the woods are big. Very big. Enormous.

The Ride

The lane out of Carhampton soon turns into one of those wide stone tracks that asks the question – just how far can you ride up this without a dab? Drop down to the car park at Nutcombe Bottom, soon entering the conifer plantation and a series of wide stone tracks that are great for side-by-side conversations, if you have any spare energy left over from the 320m climb, taking you to the highest point in the forest. The views from the eastern edge of the forest are massive: east towards the Quantocks and north across the Bristol Channel to Wales. A fast and furious descent, with one short climb to break it into two, drops you down 350m back in Carhampton, the last part on the loose stones of Hill Lane.

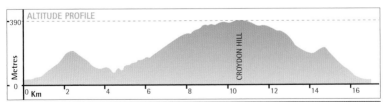

ALTITUDE PROFILE

390

Metres

0

0 Km   2   4   6   8   10   12   14   16

CROYDON HILL

CARHAMPTON & CROYDON HILL **GRADE:** ▲

TOTAL DISTANCE: 17KM » **TOTAL ASCENT**: 520M » **TIME**: 1.5–2.5 HOURS » **START/FINISH**: CARHAMPTON, SOUTHEAST OF MINEHEAD » **START GRID REF**: ST 008426 » **SATNAV**: TA24 6LP » **PARKING**: CAR PARK IN CENTRE OF CARHAMPTON **OS MAP**: EXPLORER OL9 » **PUB**: BUTCHERS ARMS, CARHAMPTON, TEL: 01643 821 333 » **CAFÉ**: BRING SANDWICHES

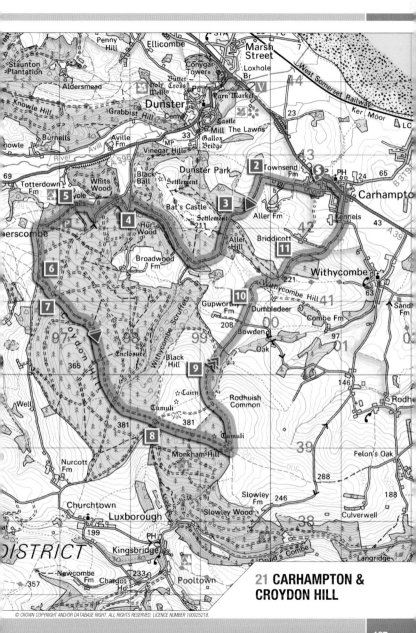

21 CARHAMPTON & CROYDON HILL

Directions – Carhampton & Croydon Hill

⮕ Exit Carhampton car park onto the A39, turn **R** then **L** opposite Carhampton Stores onto High Street signposted *Village Hall*. At the T-junction at the end of High Street turn **R**.

2 Ignore turns to right and left. Continue past the *No Through Road* sign. The tarmac turns to track. At a 4-way junction and wooden post continue **SA** signposted *Byway to Withycombe & Hill Gate*.

3 Climb on a broad stone and red earth track. At the next 4-way sign continue **SA** signposted *Public Path to Bonniton*. Soon start descending. At a fork bear **R** on the upper track. Stay on the main track, ignoring another left turn then a right turn, eventually following a stream to your left.

4 At the T-junction with the road turn **L** then after 150m take the first track on the **R** signposted *Nutcombe Bottom Car Park*. Emerge at the car park. At the T-junction with the road turn **L** uphill, **ignoring** the track directly opposite. Climb steeply then after 300m take the broad stone track uphill to the **R** towards a wooden barrier.

5 Go round the wooden barrier and bear **L**. Follow a sign for Timberscombe. After a muddy section and a short, steep, rooty climb turn **R** uphill on a broad stone forest road. At a T-junction turn **R** to continue uphill towards an orange arrow about 30m away.

6 After 800m, opposite a metal field gate set in a stone bank wall on the right (leading into sheep pasture), turn **L** uphill on the **third** wide stone forest track to the left, waymarked by an orange arrow (SS 966414).

7 At a crossroads with a lane go **SA** onto the track opposite. Shortly after the first summit at a 4-way wooden post, continue **SA** signposted '*Bridleway to Perley Combe*'.

8 After 700m at 5-way signpost continue **SA** signposted *Druids Combe*. Ignore a forest road to the right, continue **SA** towards Rodhuish Common. At a 4-way post at the edge of the woodland follow the main track round to the **L** signposted *Bridleway to Dunster* (SS 995389).

9   At the T-junction with a broad stone track turn **R**. **Easy to miss:** after 800m, having gone round a sweeping right-hand bend and at the start of a left-hand bend, turn **R** on a steeper downhill track (SS 993403), taking as a bearing an isolated farm with a grey roof in the distance.

10   At a crossroads with tarmac go **SA** (Gupworthy Farm is to the left). The tarmac turns to track. Descend then climb. At the T-junction at the edge of the forest in among gorse bushes bear **R** signposted *Public Path to Carhampton*.

11   Shortly, at the junction of several tracks bear **L** (i.e. **not** sharp left) on the lower track signposted *Carhampton*. Largely loose stone descent on a sunken track. At the road bear **L** then at the T-junction with the A39 turn **L** to return to the car park in Carhampton.

◀◉◎◎ Making a day of it
The nearest base for other rides described in the book is Porlock, west from Carhampton along the A39.

22 Monksilver & Brompton Ralph

19km

Introduction

Tucked into the eastern corner of the National Park, this ride just gets better and better as it goes on and the final descent into Monksilver will have you gagging to come back and do it again.

The Ride

A steep road climb at the start with fine views east to the Quantocks brings you to Ashbeer and the first off-road descent, steep and fast at the end. Meander your way down Somerset lanes to the hamlet of Brompton Ralph and the start of the next track – one of those smooth bedrock trails that must have seen the wheels of a thousand farm waggons in times past. Climb to the mast, follow tracks past Sedgeborough and Fryan Farms through to the busy(ish) B3224 where you may wish to turn left for 5 minutes to refuel at Ralegh's Cross Inn. If not, prepare for the best bit of the ride, first the amazing views west to the folds and combes and patchwork of fields of the National Park, then the wonderful woodland descent, dropping 200m back into Monksilver.

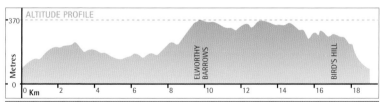

MONKSILVER & BROMPTON RALPH

GRADE: ▲

TOTAL DISTANCE: 19KM » **TOTAL ASCENT**: 400M » **TIME**: 1.5–2.5 HOURS » **START/FINISH**: MONKSILVER, SOUTHEAST OF MINEHEAD » **START GRID REF**: ST 075375 » **SATNAV**: MONKSILVER » **PARKING**: MONKSILVER COMMUNITY HALL CAR PARK, ON THE STOGUMBER ROAD ON THE SOUTHEAST EDGE OF THE VILLAGE » **OS MAP**: EXPLORER OL9 **PUB**: NOTLEY ARMS, MONKSILVER, TEL: 01984 656 217 » **CAFÉ**: RALEGH'S CROSS INN, 1.3KM WEST OF ROUTE ALONG THE B3224 TEL: 01984 640 343

22 MONKSILVER & BROMPTON RALPH

Directions – Monksilver & Brompton Ralph

⑤▸ From the Community Hall car park turn **L** uphill. After 500m **ignore** a lane on the right by a triangle of grass, then Combe Cross Lane to the left. Continue climbing.

2 Just beyond the brow of the hill and the mast, bear **R** at a T-junction by a triangle of grass signposted *Elworthy*. After 250m, immediately after a thatched house on the right, turn **R** onto a broad stone track signposted *Byway to Elworthy*.

3 Climb on a broad, sunken, grassy track, at times a bit overgrown, then descend on an earth and stone sunken track beneath overhanging trees. At the road bear **L**, soon climbing. At the crossroads with the B3224 go **SA**.

4 Long gentle descent then, after a brief climb, take the first road **R** by a gnarly old oak tree (no sign). **Ignore** a road to the right then at the T-junction turn **R** downhill.

5 Go past the church, ignoring a lane to the right, go down into Brompton Ralph then, opposite the telephone box and just before the village stores, turn **R** by a large triangle of grass and immediately **R** again onto a track climbing to the **R** of Beers Cleeve Cottage with a 'potter' outline on the wall.

6 Up and down on bedrock track. At the T-junction with the road bear **L** uphill alongside a line of telegraph poles. Climb steeply on tarmac for 1.2km, passing a small plantation of trees to the left.

7 At the T-junction at the top by a triangle of grass with a mast to your right turn **L** onto a broad gravel track.

8 At the offset crossroads with tarmac turn **L** then **R** onto similar track. The stone track turns sharp **R**, goes through a gate then becomes grass and drops down to go past a farm (Sedgeborough). Go through a stream, through a gate and up the **left-hand** field edge to the corner. Go **SA** through the newer metal gate aiming towards the far left end of the barn.

9 Join a tarmac drive and bear **L** past Fryan Farm buildings. At the T-junction with the lane turn **L**. At the T-junction with the B3224 turn **L** signposted *Ralegh's Cross* then after 250m take the first road to the **R** signposted *Colton Lane*.

10 After almost 1km, on a sharp right-hand bend, go **SA** through a small wooden bridlegate onto a track signposted *Bridleway to Sticklepath*. Stay on the right-hand edge of the field as vast views open up to the left down to the hamlets of Leighland Chapel and Stamborough.

11 Go through the gate following blue waymarks then through a second gate leading into the woodland and onto a good stone track. As this track turns downhill on a sharp left-hand hairpin bend, bear **R** slightly uphill signposted *Monksilver via Colton Cross*.

12 At a T-junction with a broader track at the top of the climb go **SA** through the gate ahead into and across the field (blue waymarks) to a gate onto the road. Turn **L**. At a T-junction by a triangle of grass go **SA** into woodland through a wooden field gate signposted *Wildlife Conservation Area, Bridleway to Monksilver*.

13 Great descent! At the T-junction with the road by Lime Walk Cottage turn **R**. At the T-junction with the main road through the village turn **R**. Ignore a no through road to the left then shortly, on a sharp right-hand bend, bear **L** signposted *Stogumber* to climb back to the car park at the start.

←💬 Making a day of it
No rides are nearby: jump back in the car and head west to Carhampton (page 135), or east to the Quantocks (page 146), just as close by.

SECTION 3

Quantocks

The Quantocks. Where every track is a bridleway, every bridleway is singletrack and every singletrack is a little twisty, turny bit of heaven. OK, so technically that might be a slight exaggeration. But it doesn't feel like one.

Have fun – it's hard not to.

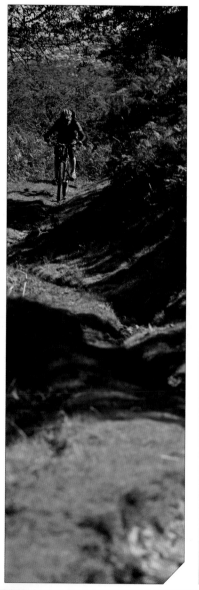

QUANTOCKS AREA MAP & ROUTE FINDER

Quantocks
Extra Riding

With their friendly feel, small size and huge bridleway network, the Quantocks encourage exploration. We do too, so here are a few pointers to help you on your way.

A Note on Start/Finish Points

You can start from virtually any village at the base of the hills. If you want to begin on a high, there are car parks at the top of the ridge on the Nether Stowey/Crowcombe Road, at the Triscombe Stone and above Weacombe. The rides in this book give directions from Holford, but can easily be started elsewhere.

Great Ridge

If you want a really easy – and fun – route, try the Great Ridge. Running along the spine of the Quantocks, it offers a pleasant, 'cruisy' ride, incredible views, wild ponies and picnic spots. Park at the Triscombe Stone, Dead Woman's Ditch or Crowcombe Park Gate and ride west. Stick to the most obvious track at all times and go for as long as you like (or until you reach the A39) before retracing your steps.

Western Quantocks

It's definitely worth exploring the western end of the Quantocks – there's a huge amount to find and the rides in this guide use our favourite trails, which aren't necessarily yours. Beginning right at the end, there's a worthwhile descent west of, and parallel to, Smith's Combe. From the bottom, head east towards Pardlestone for more singletrack and a tough climb back up. You could easily modify the *Quantocks Classic Singletrack* route using these, perhaps finishing with one of the descents from Longstone Hill into Hodder's Combe. These are relatively obstacle free, but worryingly steep and fast.

Holford

Staying around Holford, all the bridleways into Holford and Hodder's Combes make great descents. Black Hill – the ridge separating the two – has an easy grassy trail with impressive views running down

its length. It's great if you want a fast, but technically easy descent or climb. Try dropping off into Hodder's Combe for a rocky challenge, or into Holford Combe for singletrack.

Southern Quantocks

Hopping over the ridge, the descents off the southern side of the Quantocks tend to be more open, grassier and steeper than those in the northern combes. Weacombe and Bicknoller excepted, there's not much singletrack, but plenty of high speed blasting instead. Stay around Paradise Farm for grassy riding, or head to the byway descent from Triscombe for a wide and rocky trail that is recommended by many.

Great Wood

For something completely different, explore the Great Wood. While its bridleways are mainly wide forest roads, the ever-generous Forestry Commission has allowed various tracks and runs to be built. For various reasons, we can't reveal exactly where they are, but if you were to park at the Triscombe Stone and head north with your eyes open, you might find something fun. We'd also suggest you keep your eyes peeled on our 'killer' (p171) as it loops through the woods.

Cothelstone Hill

While the 'best' riding in the Quantocks may be in the west, there's plenty to explore at the other end, around Cothelstone Hill. We've left it out of this guide as the riding isn't as 'Quantock-like' as the stuff that's made the region famous, but that doesn't mean it isn't worth a look. It's quiet and the descent southeast off Cothelstone Hill always puts a smile on our faces. If you fancy it, the area's bridleways form an obvious loop which rides best anti-clockwise.

DROPPING INTO SHEPPARD'S COMBE

23 Quantocks Quickie
– Holford & Sheppard's Combe

12km

Introduction

We had trouble with this route. It rides well in both directions, which is always problematic when writing a guidebook. Which way's best? Ridden anti-clockwise, the initial climb's friendly enough, the cruise along the ridge drops slowly and the descent is good and rough – it's a fun ride. Taken clockwise, the climb is steeper and harder and the middle section trends uphill, (although the view takes your mind off that). But – and this was the decider – the descent encompasses everything that's good about riding in the Quantocks. Singletrack all the way, it's fast and it flows. It's just tricky enough to be interesting, but never so much as to scare you onto the brakes. It doesn't get much better than this!

So there it is: a route that rides well in both directions. Try both and see which way round you prefer.

The Ride

A steep climb, a big view and a fantastic singletrack descent – this ride sums up the Quantocks in a nutshell! Although short, it's not particularly easy. (Apart from the panoramic cruise along the Great Ridge and some bland forest roads in the Great Wood, there's not much in the Quantocks that is easy.) It begins with a fun ride up Holford Combe, hopping to and fro across the stream (it's easier on the right bank, more interesting on the left). This ends in a big, rough climb leading up, via some enjoyable singletrack, to the Quantock ridge and a couple of kilometres of easy riding, wild ponies and wonderful views. Then, from nowhere, a steep singletrack drops into Sheppard's Combe, accelerating easily into a long series of sweeping turns that run for a full two kilometres, only ending when you splash through the stream and into Hodder's Combe.

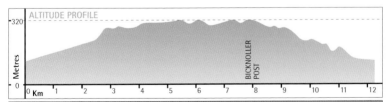

ALTITUDE PROFILE

Metres — 320 — 0

0 Km 1 2 3 4 5 6 7 8 9 10 11 12

BICKNOLLER POST

QUANTOCKS QUICKIE
GRADE: ▲ » ▲

TOTAL DISTANCE: 12KM » TOTAL ASCENT: 370M » TIME: 1.5–3 HOURS » START/FINISH: CAR PARK BY THE GREEN IN HOLFORD » START GRID REF: ST 154411 » SATNAV: HOLFORD » PARKING: FREE CAR PARK IN HOLFORD/LAYBY ON A39 OS MAP: EXPLORER 140 » PUB: THE PLOUGH, HOLFORD, TEL: 01278 741 232 » CAFÉ: SNACK VAN IN LAYBY ON A39; COMBE HOUSE HOTEL, HOLFORD, TEL: 01278 741 382

Directions – Quantocks Quickie
– Holford & Sheppard's Combe

➐ Turn **R** out of the car park and onto the road. At the T-junction, turn sharp **R** (almost back on yourself) and then keep **SA**. Follow the road up past the hotel into the woods. Keep **SA** across a grassy area and then follow the stream up the combe (pick one of the many tracks weaving around – the easier riding is on the right-hand bank (looking upstream), while the more 'interesting' stuff is on the left).

2 Eventually, cross the stream into a second grassy area. **Ignore** tracks to the right and keep **L**, crossing the stream once more. **Ignore** the track immediately to the left and take the obvious wide track ahead of you that climbs in a straight line up the side of the valley. Follow the track up and around to the left (it widens considerably) until you reach the top and a T-junction. Turn **R** and ride a short distance to the road.

3 Go **SA** across the road onto the obvious singletrack. **Ignoring** turnings, follow this to a second road and turn **R**. After a few metres, turn **L** into a car park and then immediately **R** onto singletrack running parallel to the road. Follow this to a second car park at Dead Women's Ditch.

4 Move onto the road and then, almost immediately after the car park, bear **R** onto a wide track (complete with ponies). It can be confusing up here, as there are tracks everywhere, many of which run parallel to one another and which aren't on the map. Luckily, the track you want here is always the most obvious, so don't worry too much.

Ignoring all turnings, continue **SA** along this wide track for 4km. Drop down a short, steep descent and follow the track around the head of a broad valley (views to the right). **Ignore** a turning to the left as you begin to climb gently. As the climb flattens and the trig point comes into view ahead (a fair way off!), look out for the Bicknoller Post on the right.

5 Turn **R** at the post, and then immediately **R** again (effectively back on yourself). Go **SA** across a grassy area and over two tracks. Drop steeply into the combe ahead on an initially invisible but then very obvious track. A steep start leads onto fast singletrack – watch the blind corners! As you reach the bottom of the combe, keep **L** to join (and cross) the stream. Ignoring any turnings that climb the sides of valley, weave alongside the stream to a gate, and the car park.

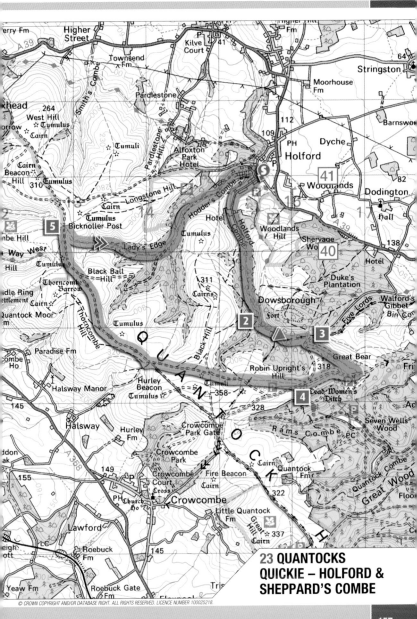

23 QUANTOCKS QUICKIE – HOLFORD & SHEPPARD'S COMBE

Introduction

The Quantock Hills are one of the best places to ride in the UK, and this route shows why. It contains three descents – Smith's Combe, Weacombe Combe and Somerton Combe – which are absolutely superb singletrack runs. Taken alone, each would be the highlight of virtually any ride, anywhere. Certainly, each could claim to be the best bridleway descent in the Quantocks. And, given that the Quantocks are such a good riding destination, these descents must be among the best in the country. Therefore, this ride contains three of the best descents in the country. And in all probability, no other ride contains so many descents of that stature. So, logically(!), this must be the best route in the UK.

The Ride

On paper this route doesn't look much, being relatively short (18km) and without much climbing (760m). But you shouldn't judge a book by its cover or a ride by its numbers. There's barely a flat metre here and the climbs all feel steeper than the descents (more efficient, see?). Anyway, the ride: a dirt track meanders out of the car park and up Hodder's Combe to the singletrack climb that leads to open ground and the Bicknoller Post. The three afore-mentioned descents follow. First, it's Smith's Combe, combining rocky madness with, quite literally, roller-coaster singletrack. Then Weacombe Combe, with its perfect sweeping singletrack turns, follows after a breath-takingly-steep climb. Finally, after a granny ring pull up Bicknoller Hill, comes Somerton Combe. Beginning flat-out across open hillside, it twists through the heather and over a fallen tree before jerking around a hairpin and dropping into Hodder's Combe. A series of sweeping bends and river crossings run almost all the way back to the car park and to the end of one of the best rides in the Quantocks.

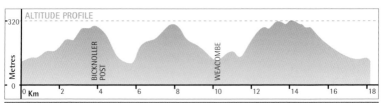

ALTITUDE PROFILE

BICKNOLLER POST

WEACOMBE

Metres

0 Km   2   4   6   8   10   12   14   16   18

QUANTOCKS CLASSIC SINGLETRACK   GRADE: ▲

TOTAL DISTANCE: 18KM » **TOTAL ASCENT:** 760M » **TIME:** 2–4 HOURS » **START/FINISH:** CAR PARK BY GREEN IN HOLFORD
START GRID REF: ST 154411 » **SATNAV:** HOLFORD » **PARKING:** FREE CAR PARK IN HOLFORD/LAYBY ON A39
OS MAP: EXPLORER 140 » **PUB:** THE PLOUGH, HOLFORD, TEL: 01278 741 232 » **CAFÉ:** SNACK VAN IN LAYBY ON A39;
COMBE HOUSE HOTEL, HOLFORD, TEL: 01278 741 382

24 **QUANTOCKS**
CLASSIC SINGLETRACK

Directions – Quantocks Classic Singletrack

➡ Turn **L** up the wide dirt track running between the car park and the green. Go through the gate and, as the track splits, fork **R** off the stone track and on to dirt. Go **SA** over the stone track then continue **SA** through the gate to follow the track up the valley alongside the river.

2 About 1km beyond the gate, the track splashes across the stream to a fork (for reference, if you look left, there is a track running straight up the hill). Fork **R**, and then keep **R** again at a second fork. Cross the stream and follow the track gently uphill. This turns to singletrack as you climb up the combe, becoming steep at the end.

3 At the top, continue **SA** across a grassy area to the Bicknoller Post. Go **SA**/slightly **R** on to the wide, sandy/stony track that runs along the ridge. As the track splits three ways, keep **SA** on the middle track and continue uphill, ignoring turnings. Don't climb to the trig point, but ride beneath it, keeping to the right-hand of the two parallel tracks. As you begin to descend, look for a wide track coming in from the right. As you merge with this, turn sharp **R** to pick up a vague grassy track heading downhill towards a plantation.

Drop your saddle for a grass-to-rock-to-rollercoaster-singletrack descent. Watch the corners – some are totally blind and it's easy to miss people coming the other way!

4 At the bottom, turn **R** and cross the stream via the ford or small bridge. Climb steeply uphill on the loose track (give it a shot – you might be surprised!). At the top, turn **R** and climb over grass until you reach a wide track. Turn **R**, then bear **L** at the fork to return to the Bicknoller Post.

5 Go **SA** past the post. Cross the main track and immediately bear **R** to descend an obvious track heading down the centre of the combe. Endless singletrack runs downhill, eventually passing through a gate and onto a wider track through the woods. Go through a second gate, out of the woods and then quickly turn **L** onto a signed bridleway.

6 Follow this into the next valley and continue **SA** until a short descent leads to a narrow bridge and a T-junction. Turn **L** to climb up Bicknoller Combe. As the track becomes vague near the top, keep roughly **SA** over a crossroads (it doesn't matter too much if you drift leftwards). Once at the top, continue **SA** over a grassy track to second, wider and stonier, track. Turn **R**.

7 Follow the trail around the head of a wide valley (views to the left!). Climb slightly and then descend towards a track junction at the Halsway Post. Fork **L** then, after about 20m, turn **L** onto grassy singletrack.

This soon turns to obvious and superb singletrack running across open land, into the bracken and then switching back on itself into the woods. Pop over the fallen tree, keep **R** at the switchback and splash through the stream.

From here, there are multiple tracks and lines joining and rejoining one another. Keep roughly **SA** and it doesn't matter which you pick – just don't climb the valley sides – and you'll end up retracing your steps through the gate and out to the car park.

25 Aisholt & the Southern Combes

16km

Introduction

The Quantocks can be split into four parts. At the western end, there's the open singletrack and steep combe riding that everyone associates with the word 'Quantocks'. Further east, the Great Wood offers easy forest roads, hidden single-track and downhill runs. Right at the far end, towards the M5, is the area around Cothelstone Hill, full of sunken tracks and country lanes. And in between these last two lie the appropriately named *Middle Hill* and the village of Aisholt. Here, the trails are wider and often bordered by hedges and the heathery hillsides are replaced by grass and woodland. Not often ridden by visiting (or local) mountain bikers, it's a little different – and significantly quieter – than the usual Quantocks fare.

The Ride

Technically, this isn't too hard a ride, although you do have to work for your fun. Quiet lanes and a long, tough-ish climb carry you from Hawkshead Reservoir up onto the hills. You'll want to pause for a moment at the top as the view stretches south for miles. A relatively straight and wide, but rocky, steep and often muddy descent plunges to West Bagborough and the pub. Keep an eye on what you eat and drink though, or the climb back up will feel even longer and steeper than it's already going to. Once back atop the ridge, you've got a choice. If it's been dry, and you fancy some singletrack, a long, fast run that's as good as anything in this guide swoops down into the centre of the valley. If it's been muddy, or you like going fast with the wind in your hair, stick to the edge of the Great Wood for over 2km of high-speed rattling!

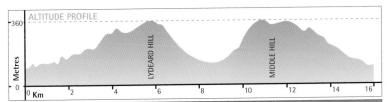

ALTITUDE PROFILE

Metres

LYDEARD HILL

MIDDLE HILL

Km 2 4 6 8 10 12 14 16

AISHOLT & THE SOUTHERN COMBES

GRADE: ▲

TOTAL DISTANCE: 16KM » **TOTAL ASCENT**: 580M » **TIME**: 1.5–3 HOURS » **START/FINISH**: HAWKRIDGE RESERVOIR CAR PARK, SOUTHWEST OF SPAXTON » **START GRID REF**: ST 206361 » **SATNAV**: SPAXTON (CLOSEST) **PARKING**: HAWKRIDGE RESERVOIR CAR PARK » **OS MAP**: EXPLORER 140 » **PUB**: RISING SUN INN, WEST BAGBOROUGH, TEL: 01823 432 575 » **CAFÉ**: SANDWICH TIME

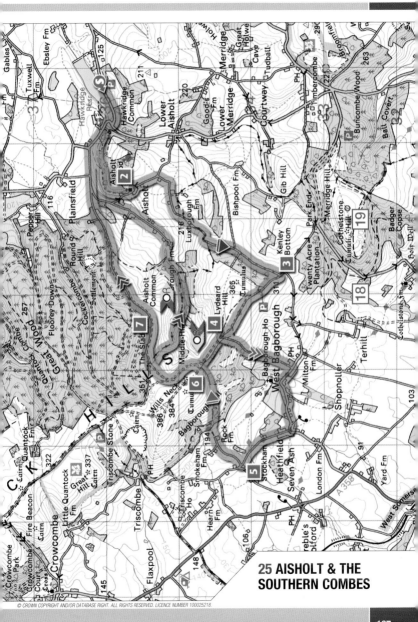

25 AISHOLT & THE SOUTHERN COMBES

Directions – Aisholt & the Southern Combes

❶ From the car park by Hawkridge Reservoir follow the road westwards with the water to your right. At the T-junction turn **R**, signed to *Over Stowey*. Cross the dam wall then turn **L** downhill by a house called *Martindale*. Follow bridleway signposts onto a climbing track ahead.

② At the road, turn **L** steeply uphill, passing Aisholt Church. Soon after the gradient eases, turn first **R** uphill onto a no through road. The tarmac turns to track. Continue climbing to the top with great views opening up on either side.

③ At the T-junction with the road, turn **R** onto a parallel wooded track signed *Bridleway*. Go through the car park onto the obvious wide stone track beyond the gate with fantastic views to the south and west.

④ *After 800m, go through a gate and turn **L** steeply downhill by a red arrow signposted *Vehicles*. Drop fast down a loose descent with several round concrete pipes across the path. The track drops to the *Rising Sun Inn* in West Bagborough. Turn **R** on the road for 1km, pass a telephone box and then turn first **R** onto a road called *Heathfield*, signed to *Triscombe*.

> **OR** * SHORTCUT
>
> Or, after 800m, continue **SA** on a wide track. Rejoin main route at point 6.

⑤ After a further 1km, take the first road to the **R**, signed with an '!'(!). Keep going as the tarmac turns to track. Go through the gate and fork **R** onto a steep and stony track. After crossing a forestry track the surface becomes easier and the gradient slightly less steep.

⑥ Emerge from the woodland onto a wide open grassy heather area with gravel tracks. Continue **SA** (ignore the obvious track to the left) and contour around the hillside. At a fork of tracks, bear **R** towards the forest, then follow this track alongside the woodland, with the trees to your left*.

▶OR▶
* OPTIONAL SINGLETRACK FINISH (DRY WEATHER ONLY)

As you reach the trees, turn **R** just after a low broken wall/bank. Drop fast over grass and onto singletrack, heading for the bottom of the valley. Swoop through singletrack and, as it ends, continue **SA** onto a wider track. Keep **SA** once again onto tarmac. Head down the lane, ignoring bridleway turnings. Keep **L** at the junction. At the next junction, keep **R**, rejoining the main route (which comes in from the left).

7 Rattle gently but rapidly downhill on a wide stone track. The track turns to tarmac. Continue downhill in the same direction. At the T-junction by a road signpost, turn **R** towards *Taunton, Bridgwater*. Rejoin your outward route and turn **L** after crossing the dam wall to return to the car park.

CLIMBING BACK UP AFTER SMITH'S COMBE

26 Quantocks Killer Loop

27km

Introduction

The observant among you will have noticed that this ride is pretty much just a mixture of the Quantocks Quickie (p155) and Classic Singletrack (p159) routes with a loop through the Great Wood tacked on to the end. We make only a slight apology for that. In such a small area as the Quantocks, routes are always going to have to share bridleways to some extent – and the stuff that's been reused is so good that we'd happily ride it twice in one day, let alone on two different routes! If you've already ridden the two routes mentioned above, you'll know exactly what we mean and will be pretty excited about this longer version. If, however, you do fancy exploring the area a bit more, turn to page 152 for a few suggestions on how to alter and modify this route.

The Ride

This route crosses and re-crosses itself throughout its 27km length – as is the nature of Quantock riding. This means that it's easy to shorten or adapt. The first 'loop' of the ride contains the spicy Smith's Combe, the fast Weacombe and the single-track beneath Lady's Edge – three fantastic descents, each with a tough climb preceding it. A steep climb (push?) and quick descent lead into the second section – a tough climb out of Holford Combe, some decent single-track and an entertaining cruise to the Triscombe Stone. A run through the Great Wood on wide bridleways is next. These aren't bad to ride, but we'd recommend you keep your eyes peeled for singletrack instead – there's some good stuff around here and you shouldn't be afraid to explore! Once out of the trees, there's a chance to admire the view before a final singletrack blast down Somerton Combe and a splashy, swoopy run to the finish.

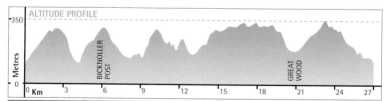

ALTITUDE PROFILE

Metres — 350 ... 0

BICKNOLLER POST

GREAT WOOD

0 Km 3 6 9 12 15 18 21 24 27

QUANTOCKS KILLER LOOP

GRADE:

TOTAL DISTANCE: 27KM » **TOTAL ASCENT:** 1,100M » **TIME:** 3–6 HOURS » **START/FINISH:** CAR PARK BY GREEN IN HOLFORD » **START GRID REF:** ST 154411 » **SATNAV:** HOLFORD » **PARKING:** FREE CAR PARK IN HOLFORD/LAYBY ON A39 **OS MAP:** EXPLORER 140 » **PUB:** THE PLOUGH, HOLFORD, TEL: 01278 741 232 » **CAFÉ:** SNACK VAN IN LAYBY ON A39; COMBE HOUSE HOTEL, HOLFORD, TEL: 01278 741 382

SMITH'S COMBE

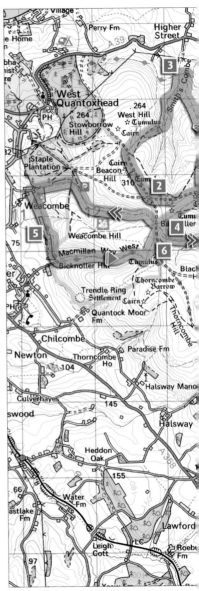

26 QUANTOCKS KILLER LOOP

Directions – Quantocks Killer Loop

➏ Head out of the car park and turn **L** along the road, alongside the green. Shortly beyond the green, continue **SA** onto a wide track as the road bears to the right (beside the ancient dog pound). Climb steadily through the woods. Keep **R** at the fork and continue onto open ground. Continue in the same direction, ignoring turnings until you reach a fork – keep **R** (on the wider of the two tracks) and begin to descend. Climb a short rise and continue **SA** to a junction of wide tracks.

2 Turn **R**, then at the next junction, keep **SA** on the right-hand of the two parallel tracks (don't climb towards the trig point). Descend gradually until a wide track merges from the right. As it does so, turn sharp **R** onto grass to pick up a vague track heading downhill towards a plantation. Drop your saddle for a grass-to-rock-to-rollercoaster-singletrack-with-stream-crossings descent. Watch the corners – some are totally blind and it's only too easy to miss people coming the other way!

3 At the bottom, turn **R** and cross the stream via the ford or small bridge. Climb steeply uphill. At the top, turn **R** and climb over grass until you reach a wide track (yes, you've been here before!). Turn **R**, then bear **L** at the fork (you went right last time) to return to the Bicknoller Post.

4 Continue **SA** past the post, across the main track and then immediately bear **R** to descend an obvious grassy track heading down the centre of the combe. Endless singletrack runs downhill, eventually passing through a gate and onto a wider track through the woods. Go through a second gate, out of the woods and then quickly turn **L** onto a signed bridleway.

5 Follow this into the next valley and continue **SA** until a short descent leads to a narrow bridge and a T-junction. Turn **L** to climb up Bicknoller Combe. Almost at the top of the climb, turn **L** at a track crossroads. Continue **SA** over tracks and grass until you reach the wide, sandy ridge track. Turn **L** and follow the track until you return to the Bicknoller Post.

6 Turn **R** at the post, and then immediately **R** again (effectively back on yourself) onto grass. Go **SA** across a grassy area and over two tracks. Drop steeply into the combe ahead on an obvious track. Fire down the steep section and into speedy singletrack

– watch the blind corners! As you reach the bottom of the combe, keep **L** to join (and cross) the stream. Follow the track downstream, to a second stream crossing. Turn **R**, and begin to climb the very obvious track running straight up the hillside opposite. It might be a bit of a push...

7 At the top, continue **SA** over the grass ridge and then **SA** into the combe on the other side – quickly descending onto obvious singletrack. Cross the stream and bear **R** across the grassy clearing onto an obvious track. Follow this into the trees and pick one of the many tracks weaving across the stream. The easier riding is on the right-hand bank (looking upstream), while the more 'interesting' stuff is on the left. Just follow the stream uphill and you'll be ok.

8 Eventually, cross the stream into a second grassy area. Ignoring tracks to the right, keep hard **L**, crossing the stream once more and then, ignoring the track immediately to the left, continue up the wide track ahead of you, climbing in a straight line up the side of the valley. Keep going roughly **SA** until you reach the top and a T-junction. Turn **R** and ride a short distance to the road.

9 Go **SA** across the road onto obvious singletrack. Ignoring turnings, follow this to a second road and turn **R**. After a few metres, turn **L** into a car park and then immediately **R** onto singletrack running parallel to the road. Follow this to a second car park at Dead Women's Ditch. Rejoin the road and pass the car park. Almost immediately beyond it, bear **R** onto a wide track. Follow this for 1km, until a wide track comes in from the left. Bear slightly **L** across this track and onto a vague and narrow grassy trail. Follow this up and over the hill and then follow your nose down to the car park and road ahead.

10 At the road, turn **R**. Continue to the trees and turn **L** onto a wide and obvious track. Cruise along this for 2km until you reach the Triscombe Stone car park, and turn **L** into it. (It's the first car park you reach, slightly off to the left.) Go through the car park and either follow the road or move slightly **R** to pick up permissive singletrack running parallel to the road. Follow this until it rejoins the road by fences. Continue in the same direction.

Directions – Quantocks Killer Loop continued...

11 At the corner, continue **SA** onto a wide track. After a short way, turn **L** onto another wide track and descend rapidly. At the T-junction, turn **R**.

NOTE: Lots of singletrack options in this area – keep your eyes peeled along this section of the route, or stop and explore the area. If you decide to do so, just follow your nose to the bottom of the hill and to the car park.

12 At the car park, turn sharp **L** and pick up the wide track running up beside the house. Follow this, and signs for car parking, until they both swing around a wide right-hand hairpin. Continue **SA** here, climbing up and out of the woods.

13 Once back at the road, cross over and go **SA** to climb through the car park, bearing **R** immediately after doing so. Follow the wide track up and over the hillside, passing the trig point before descending around loose corners to join a wide track.

14 Turn **L** and follow this for just under 1km. A few metres before a wide track merges from the left at the Halsway Post, turn **R**.

15 Follow increasingly obvious and quality singletrack across open land, into the bracken and then switching back on itself into the woods. Cross (jump!) the fallen tree, then keep **R** at the switchback and splash through the stream.

From here, there are multiple tracks and lines joining and rejoining one another. Keep roughly **SA** and it doesn't matter which you pick – just don't climb the valley sides – and you'll end up retracing your steps through the gate and out to the car park.

THE FINAL DESCENT OF SOMERTON COMBE

Appendix

Tourist Information Centres
Dartmoor

Ashburton	T: 01364 653 426
Bovey Tracey	T: 01626 832 047
Buckfastleigh	T: 01364 644 522
Chagford	T: 01647 432 080
Ivybridge	T: 01752 897 035
Moretonhampstead	T: 01647 440 043
Newton Abbot	T: 01626 215 667
Okehampton	T: 01837 53 020
Princetown	T: 01822 890 414
Tavistock	T: 01822 612 938

Exmoor

Combe Martin	T: 01271 883 319
Dulverton	T: 01398 323 841
Lynton	T: 01598 752 225
Minehead	T: 01643 702 624
Porlock Visitor Centre	T: 01643 863 150
South Molton	T: 01769 574 122

Quantocks

Bridgwater	T: 01278 427 652
Nether Stowey	T: 01278 733 642
Taunton	T: 01823 336 344
Quantocks AONB Service	T: 01823 451 884

Weather

www.bbc.co.uk/weather
www.metoffice.gov.uk

Bike Shops
Dartmoor

Okehampton

Moor Cycles	T: 01837 659 677
Okehampton Cycles	T: 01837 532 48

Plymouth

Alltrax	T: 01752 863 533
Bike Cellar	T: 01752 408 338
Certini	T: 01752 849 315
Cogs Bikes	T: 01752 600 601
Halfords Ltd	T: 01752 224 006
	T: 01752 661 652
Natural Cycles	T: 01752 550 729
Plymouth Cycle Scene	T: 01752 257 701

Tavistock

Dartmoor Cycles	T: 01822 618 178
Tavistock Cycles	T: 01822 617 630

Exmoor & the Quantocks

Barnstaple

Bike-It	T: 01271 323 873
Bike Shed	T: 01271 328 628
Halfords	T: 01271 344 490
Planet Bike	T: 01271 327 455

Bridgwater

Bicycle Chain	T: 01278 423 640
Halfords	T: 01278 453 370
St John Street Cycles	T: 01278 441 500

Minehead

Pompy's Cycles	T: 01643 704 077

Taunton

Bicycle Chain	T: 01823 252 499
Ians Cycle Centre	T: 01823 365 917
King's Cycles	T: 01823 352 272
Ralph Colman Cycles	T: 01823 275 822
Six Cycles	T: 01823 323 130

Tiverton

Maynards Cycle Shop	T: 01884 253 979
Ron's Cycle Centre	T: 01884 255 750

Wellington

King's Cycles	T: 01823 662 260

Bike Hire
Dartmoor
Ashburton
CRS Adventures .... T: 01364 653 444

Nr Okehampton
Devon Cycle Hire .... T: 01837 861 141

Exmoor and the Quantocks
Crowcombe
Quantock Orchard
Caravan Park .... T: 01984 618 618
(You must stay on the site in order to rent)

Minehead
Exmoor Cycle Hire .... T: 01643 705 307
Pompy's Cycle .... T: 01643 704 077

Porlock
Porlock Cycle Hire .... T: 07946 832 541

Accommodation
Youth Hostels
Visit www.yha.org.uk

Dartmoor
Bellever .... T: 0845 371 9622
Okehampton .... T: 0845 371 9651

Exmoor
Exford .... T: 0845 371 9634
Minehead .... T: 0845 371 9033

Quantocks
Closest is Minehead

Other Accommodation
There are many websites listing places to stay
from bunkhouses to top hotels. Try:

Dartmoor
www.dartmooraccommodation.co.uk
www.dartmoor.co.uk
www.dartmoorsearch.co.uk

Exmoor
www.exmooraccommodation.co.uk
www.exmoor.com
www.visit-exmoor.co.uk

Quantocks
www.quantockonline.co.uk
www.somerset-accommodation.co.uk

Camping
Moorhouse Farm, just north of Holford
(has a peacock) .... T: 01278 741 295

Quantock Orchard Caravan Park,
Crowcombe .... T: 01984 618 618

Hotels, Self-catering and B&B
Old Cider House,
Nether Stowey .... T: 01278 732 228

Chilcombe Stables,
Bicknoller .... T: 01984 656 224

The Hood Arms, Kilve .... T: 01278 741 210

Bicknoller Coachhouse (sleeps 4-6),
Bicknoller .... T: 01984 656 224

GROUPS:
Campbell Farm bunkhouse, North Petherton
(nr Bridgwater) .... T: 01278 662 537

Food and Drink
See the individual listings under each ride.

Food and Drink – Quantocks
Cafés
Cafés are thin on the ground in the Quantocks.
There's the odd village shop, a snack van or two
and the up-market

Combe House Hotel,
Holford .... T: 01278 741 382

Pubs

Pubs, however, aren't thin on the ground, and there are some good 'uns!

The Carew Arms,
Crowcombe _____ T: 01984 618 631

The Blue Ball Inn,
Triscombe .... T: 01984 618 242

The Hood Arms, Kilve _____ T: 01278 741 210

The Rose & Crown,
Nether Stowey _____ T: 01278 732 265

The Rising Sun, Bagborough .. T: 01823 432 575

The Plough, Holford _____ T: 01278 741 232

Useful Websites

Dartmoor National Park Authority –
www.dartmoor-npa.gov.uk

Dartmoor Tourism – **www.discoverdartmoor.com**

Exmoor National Park Authority –
www.exmoor-nationalpark.gov.uk

Exmoor Tourism – **www.visit-exmoor.co.uk**

www.thequantockhills.co.uk

Other Publications

Mountain Biking Trail Centres – The Guide
Tom Fenton, Vertebrate Publishing
www.v-publishing.co.uk

Wales Mountain Biking – Beicio Mynydd Cymru
Tom Hutton, Vertebrate Publishing
www.v-publishing.co.uk

Cotswolds Mountain Biking – 20 Classic Rides
Tom Fenton, Vertebrate Publishing
www.v-publishing.co.uk

Dartmoor for Cyclists
A tough, detailed waterproof map showing tried and tested cycle routes, designed to help you plan your visit with confidence whether you are cycling off-road or touring. All paths and tracks where cyclists have a legal or permitted right to ride are shown. Routes have been graded and colour coded by cyclists so that you can easily identify the paths that will suit your ability and mood. The map includes enlargements of the Tamar Valley AONB and Haldon Forest Park and shows public transport hubs. Produced in cooperation with the National Park Authority.
www.harveymaps.co.uk

Croydecycle
Mike Harrison produces a series of excellent maps of Exmoor showing astonishing detail on large scale maps.
www.croydecycle.co.uk

The Author
Nick Cotton

Nick Cotton has written over 40 bike guides in the past 20 years, riding more than 30,000 miles all over Britain during the course of his research. He has travelled and trekked extensively, climbing to over 18,000ft on three continents and has cycled in Morocco and Patagonia (the worst winds in the world!).

He lives in the Lune Valley in Cumbria, between the Lakes and the Dales. He is very partial to fine coffee, real ale and cakes, especially on the course of a ride. Six feet four and 14 stones needs a lot of fuel.

The Photographer
John Coefield

As well as being Vertebrate's Publishing Manager, **John Coefield** is also an accomplished photographer with images regularly published in a variety of national publications, including **Climb Magazine**, **Climber Magazine** and numerous rock climbing guidebooks. John has been riding since a young age and these days divides his time almost equally between riding, rock climbing, photography and his young family. To view more of John's images please visit: **www.johncoefield.com**

Vertebrate Publishing

Mountain Bike Rider (MBR) Magazine called our MTB guides *"...a series of glossy, highly polished and well researched guidebooks to some of the UK's favourite riding spots."*

We want to provide you - the rider - with well-researched, informative, functional, inspirational and great-looking MTB guidebooks that document the superb riding across the length and breadth of the UK. So if you want to go riding somewhere, you can count on us to point you in the right direction.

As well as our series of MTB guidebooks, we have award-winning and bestselling titles covering a range of leisure activities, including; cycling, rock climbing, hillwalking and others. We are best known for our MTB titles, including the bestseller **Dark Peak Mountain Biking**, which **BIKEmagic.com** said was *"far and away the best Peak guide we've come across".*

Our autobiography of the British rock climbing legend **Jerry Moffatt** won the *Grand Prize* at the *2009 Banff Mountain Book Festival.*

We also produce many leading outdoor titles for other publishers including the **Mountain Leader** and **Walking Group Leader Schemes** (MLTUK) and rock climbing guidebooks for the **British Mountaineering Council** and the **Fell and Rock Climbing Club**. For more information, please visit our website: **www.v-publishing.co.uk** or email us: **info@v-publishing.co.uk**

VERTEBRATE PUBLISHING

MOUNTAIN BIKING GUIDEBOOKS

About the Great Outdoors

The great outdoors is not bottom bracket friendly; beautiful flowing singletrack can give way suddenly to scary rock gardens, hard climbs can appear right at the end of a ride and sheep will laugh at your attempts to clean your nemesis descent. Of course it's not all good news. You'll need a good bike to ride many of the routes in our set of mountain biking guides. You'll also need fuel, spare clothing, first aid skills, endurance, power, determination and plenty of nerve.

Bridleways litter our great outdoors. Our guides, written by local riders, reveal the secrets of their local area's best rides from 6 to 300km in length, including ideas for link-ups and night-riding options. Critically acclaimed, our comprehensive series of guides is the country's bestselling and most respected – purpose-built for the modern mountain biker.

The Guidebooks

Each guidebook features up to 28 rides, complete with comprehensive directions, specialist mapping and inspiring photography, all in a pocket-sized, portable format. Written by riders for riders, our guides are designed to maximise ride-ability and are full of useful local area information.

Available from bikeshops, bookshops or direct from:

www.v-publishing.co.uk

MOUNTAIN BIKING TRAIL CENTRES THE GUIDE

TOM FENTON

Mountain Biking Trail Centres – The Guide is the only comprehensive guide to the UK's network of purpose-built, off-road mountain biking trails, featuring thousands of kilometres of singletrack, cross country, downhill, freeride and bike park riding at 67 centres across England, Scotland and Wales.

Included are classics such as Dalby, Coed y Brenin and Glentress, lesser-known centres such as Balblair and Coed Trallwm, together with the latest developments including Whinlatter, Rossendale Lee Quarry and many new trails at existing centres.